American Belleek

Mary Frank Gaston

COLLECTOR BOOKS
A Division of Schroeder Publishing Co., Inc.

The current values in this book should be used only as a guide. They are not intended to set prices, which vary from one section of the country to another. Auction prices as well as dealer prices vary greatly and are affected by condition as well as demand. Neither the Author nor the Publisher assumes responsibility for any losses that might be incurred as a result of consulting this guide.

Other Books by Mary Frank Gaston

The Collector's Encyclopedia of Limoges Porcelain	$19.95
The Collector's Encyclopedia of R.S. Prussia	$24.95
Blue Willow, An Illustrated Value Guide	$9.95
The Collector's Encyclopedia of Flow Blue China	$19.95
Haviland Collectables and Objects of Art	$19.95

Add $1.00 for postage for the first book.
Copies of these books may be ordered from:

Mary Frank Gaston
P.O. Box 342
Bryan, Texas 77806

Collector Books
P.O. Box 3009
Paducah, Kentucky 42001

To Jerry and Jeremy

Acknowledgements

Without the help of several persons, this book on American Belleek would not have been possible. I thank my publisher, Bill Schroeder, Collector Books, for providing me this opportunity to present an all-color presentation of American Belleek.

I thank my husband, Jerry, for photographing all of the examples of American Belleek shown here. Jerry also helped with the research on this subject, edited the manuscript, and designed the format of the book. Jerry's own interest in American Belleek, in addition to my own, made the work on this book a very enjoyable experience.

Last, but by no means least, I thank the individuals who so generously gave of their time and knowledge to make this book a reality. Those collectors and dealers, through devoted interest and experience, supplied invaluable insights on the fascinating topic of American Belleek. They provided the beautiful examples of American Belleek featured in this book. I sincerely appreciate each one's special contribution, and I would like to take this opportunity to mention each by name:

Erma and Harry Brown, Bordentown, New Jersey
Carol Elliot, Elliot's Antiques, McAllen, Texas
Horace Mann, Houston, Texas
Mr. and Mrs. Don H. Stinchcomb, Pennington, New Jersey

The Willets Portrait Mug, decorated by Nosek, featured on the front and back cover is courtesy of Mr. and Mrs. Harry Brown.

Preface

The American Belleek Era played a special role in the history of the American porcelain industry. Porcelain identified by the name "American Belleek" represents the zenith of that industry. At no other time have American porcelain manufacturers created such works of art. Indeed the creativeness and craftsmanship exemplified by American Belleek rival any of its European counterparts.

American Belleek qualifies as a collector's item not only because such porcelain represents ceramic art made from over fifty to one hundred years ago, but also because the American Belleek Era lasted for a relatively short time--from the early 1880s until about 1930. Thus a finite amount of American Belleek is available.

The rise and fall of the American Belleek industry reflects the American scene over that period. The height of American Belleek production, the mid 1880s until about 1910, mirrors the decorative home and table styles in vogue during the late Victorian years. The down fall of the industry is seen by the changing tastes and habits of the American public preceding and following World War I. The definitive end of the Era can be marked by the beginning of the Depression years.

Porcelain made during the American Belleek Era is truly an exciting field of collecting. This book is a survey of that subject. All American companies known to have manufactured and marketed porcelain as "Belleek" are included. Brief historical information, marks, and examples are provided for each company. Current values are also quoted for the pieces illustrated.

American Belleek provides almost limitless opportunities for research and study. The aim of this book is to give greater visibility to the American Belleek Era and to encourage further study, appreciation, and knowledge of this important aspect of "Americana."

Mary Frank Gaston
P.O. Box 342
Bryan, Texas 77806

Contents

Historical Origins and Development of American Belleek

From the early 1880s until about 1930, several American potteries manufactured a special type of porcelain which they called "Belleek." Neither the porcelain nor its name originated in America, however. The porcelain body was invented by William H. Goss of Stoke-on-Trent, England, probably during the late 1850s (Barber, 1893). The commercial development and name of the porcelain actually originated in Ireland.

Belleek is the name of a small town in the Northern Ireland county of Fermanagh. A pottery was established under the name of D. McBirney & Co. in that village in 1857. Existing natural resources made the location suitable for such a business. With only a few interruptions through the years, that pottery has remained in operation from its founding until the present, although there have been changes in its ownership and directors. Since 1920, the pottery has been named the Belleek Pottery Limited (Degenhardt, 1978)

When the Irish pottery was founded, production was limited to earthenware or semi-porcelain products. The owners, David McBirney and Robert Armstrong, however, were anxious to make porcelain because porcelain is considered the highest form of the potter's art. Porcelain experiments were not successful until McBirney and Armstrong were able to hire several people away from William Goss' factory in England, including the manager, William Bromley, Sr. (Barber, 1893). It is not clear from either Barber's account or from Degenhardt's just when the English potters came to Ireland to teach Goss' technique. Degenhardt states that some parian (unglazed Belleek) was made at the Irish factory in 1863, but he notes that came about only through six years of effort. At any rate, porcelain manufacturing was perfected by 1872, because examples were shown at the Dublin Exposition that year. The Irish porcelain quickly gained great renown not only in Ireland, but in England and other parts of Europe as well. Royalty, including Queen Victoria, purchased the porcelain thereby sanctioning its merit (Degenhardt, 1978).

"Belleek" soon became the name used to identify the Irish porcelain, but that was not the intention of the factory. The company used "Belleek" in the marks on earthenware as well as on porcelain; and in fact according to Degenhardt, earthenware remained the chief production of the company until around 1920. "Belleek" was used only to refer to the location of the pottery and not to a particular form of porcelain. Today, although "Belleek" is technically defined by Webster (1982) as a type of pottery resembling porcelain, Belleek is commonly considered a special type of porcelain.

Belleek is not the same as true or hard-paste porcelain even though it is composed of similar natural ingredients and has the same two essential characteristics of hard-paste porcelain--translucency and vitreosity. Belleek and hard-paste porcelain are manufactured in different ways. Belleek becomes both vitreous and translucent in only one firing. The Belleek body is called "parian" after the first firing, and it is unglazed. Hard-paste porcelain becomes translucent but not vitreous during the first firing, and the resulting body is called "bisque" which is also unglazed. Parian and bisque are primarily used for statuary, figurines, and busts. Tableware and decorative items in both Belleek and hard-paste porcelain are usually glazed, which requires that both types of porcelain be refired. During the second firing, the glaze melts into the hard-paste bisque body making the glaze and body inseparable and vitreous (non-porous). During the second firing for the glazed parian of Belleek porcelain, the glaze does not permeate the body because the parian body is non-porous or vitrified. The glaze on Belleek actually covers the body with an overlay effect.

The glazes used on the Irish Belleek became a distinguishing characteristic of the Irish porcelain. The glazes were lustrous and irridescent like a pearl. They were patterned after the "nacreous" glaze invented by J.J.H. Brianchon, a Frenchman, in 1857. Degenhardt (1978) states that the Irish pottery purchased a patent from Brianchon in order to develop the pearl and cob luster finishes.

The unique pearl luster glazes, the thin translucent body, and the variety of distinctive shapes of the Irish porcelain established the ware as an art porcelain from its beginnings. Intricate lattice work and basket-type creations became popular as did naturalistic themes. Tree boughs or twig-shaped handles, applied floral and leaf decor, plus many items fashioned in the form of marine life including seashells, fish, dolphins, and swans, and figural designs became identifying traits of the Irish Belleek. Expert workmanship with an eye for detail can be seen on ordinary items made and decorated in extraordinary ways. A teapot might have a figural head for a spout and a twisted fish tail for a handle, or delicate seashells may form the feet and finials on objects. Irish Belleek was made to be appreciated first for its aesthetic quality; its utilitarian value was secondary.

Such high standards made the porcelain expensive in the early years. Increased technology and modernization during the twentieth century made Irish Belleek more affordable, but the fine quality and craftsmanship have not been sacrificed.

Porcelain made by the Irish Belleek Pottery Limited is known and appreciated all over the world. "Belleek" brings to mind the image of Ireland in the same manner as the Blarney Stone, St. Patrick's Day, and shamrocks. It is to this company and the name of its site that we owe the origins of American Belleek. (For a complete history of the Belleek Pottery, see Richard Degenhardt, *Belleek: The Collector's Guide and Illustrated Reference*, 1978).

Irish Belleek was first exhibited in the United States at the Philadelphia Exposition in 1876 (Reilly, 1952). Examples, must have been seen by Americans prior to that time, however, because Boger (1971, p. 28) states that one Trenton, New Jersey, pottery (Ott & Brewer) displayed an ivory porcelain decorated to look like the Irish Belleek at the same Exposition. Ott & Brewer must have admired the Irish porcelain very much to imitate it. Although Ott & Brewer were successful in making parian (which was also exhibited at the 1876 Exposition) and ivory porcelain, the owners were not completely satisfied with their attempts at duplicating the Irish Belleek. This is evident because in 1882, six years after the Exposition, they found it necessary to hire William Bromley, Jr., from the Irish pottery to teach them the technique. William's father, William Bromley, Sr., had been instrumental in developing the Irish porcelain. Eventually, it was he who was responsible for perfecting the process for Ott & Brewer. William, Sr., came to Trenton the next year (in 1883) with some other potters from the Irish factory because his son was not able to implement the technique himself (Barber, 1893).

With the senior Bromley's expertise, Ott & Brewer was able to produce a porcelain with the same characteristics of the Irish Belleek: a thin translucent body, light in weight, with a pearly, irridescent glaze. Barber (1893) states that Ott & Brewer porcelain was "fully equal" to the Irish Belleek, and that in color and lightness of weight, the products were "superior."

Other Trenton companies were eager to follow Ott & Brewer's example in making porcelain like the Irish. In fact, William Bromley, Sr., went to work for the Willets Manufacturing Company after developing the Belleek porcelain for Ott & Brewer. Thus from a chain of events, with one common denominator, William Bromley, Sr., "Belleek" porcelain spread from England to Ireland to America and within America to several different companies. In addition to Bromley, other Irish workers came to work for the American factories in Trenton. Local persons trained at Ott & Brewer or Willets went on to work for other Trenton potteries, and some eventually took Belleek production to Ohio. An inner network developed which was actually responsible for Belleek porcelain being made in the United States long after Ott & Brewer closed its doors. It is not surprising that many of the shapes and decorations of American Belleek made by the different companies are similar not only to the Irish Belleek but to each other as well.

Ott & Brewer was unquestionably the first American pottery to make American Belleek, but that fact may not be totally clear because of misleading information found in the biography of Walter Scott Lenox written by George Sanford Holmes in 1924. Holmes shows a picture of an ornately designed pitcher in the form of a shell with a figure applied at the top of the handle. The caption of that photograph reads: "The first piece of Belleek made in America." Schwartz (1970, Plate 254) illustrates the same piece and identifies it as designed by Walter Lenox and in fact signed "W.S.L./1887." Schwartz states that the piece was made while Lenox was working at Ott & Brewer. Barber (1893, p.233) shows the same example with the caption, "Shell and Cupid." Barber attributes the piece to the Willets Manufacturing Company. Walter Lenox worked as an art director at both Ott & Brewer and at Willets before forming the Ceramic Art Company in 1889 with Jonathan Coxon, Sr., which eventually became Lenox, Inc..

Robinson and Feeny (1980, p.41) indicate that Lenox worked at Ott & Brewer before going to Willets, but no dates are provided. Thus there is conflicting information on just where the item was executed. Nevertheless, the shell pitcher was definitely not the first piece of American Belleek ever made, even if it was made at Ott & Brewer. It may have been the first piece of American Belleek designed by Walter Lenox if the item was made at Ott & Brewer. If the pitcher was made at Willets as Barber says, then it was surely not the first American Belleek ever designed by Walter Lenox.

Holmes' account of the Lenox story is quite biased. He implies that Lenox, with the help of two Irish Belleek potters, did develop the first American Belleek. He does note that Lenox worked for Ott & Brewer and Willets, but he does not credit those companies as having made American Belleek. Holmes (1924, p.18) negates any American ceramic production by saying that during the time Lenox was at Ott & Brewer, that ". . . there was little of the artistic in the American ceramic products of that period." Holmes continues (p. 18) that Lenox wanted to "give vent to his own aspirations and individuality," and thus in 1889 Walter Lenox and Jonathan Coxon, Sr., formed the Ceramic Art Company. Holmes goes on to say (pp. 23 and 24), that Lenox tried unsuccessfully for a long time to make a ware like the Irish Belleek; but, he concludes, "finally failure gave way to perfection and the result was a china which charmed by the warmth and glow of its coloring and ranked in richness and quality with the masterpieces of other lands. Today, the first piece of Belleek turned out in America is a treasured exhibit in the display room of the Lenox pottery."

It is understandable from that statement how readers would assume that Lenox made the first piece of American Belleek and, from the caption of the photograph, infer that the Shell pitcher was that very first piece. Some antique guides do state that Walter Lenox of Lenox, Inc. was the first to make American Belleek.

Their source of information was evidently Holmes' biography. Walter Lenox did play a great part in the development of the American porcelain industry, but the earlier contributions of Ott & Brewer and Willets must not be overshadowed by that later company.

After 1883 until about 1930, several companies successfully manufactured American Belleek. The first companies making Belleek in Trenton used the word "Belleek" in the marks on the porcelain. That term or designation was continued by the later companies which made a similar type of porcelain. To the manufacturers, the word "Belleek" identified a particular type of porcelain--not merely a town in Ireland where a pottery was located. The use of the word began as an attempt to tell the public that the porcelain was the same or as good as the Irish porcelain. At that particular time in history, Americans were quite prejudiced against local pottery and porcelain. Most buyers thought quality ware could be made only in Europe.

The American Belleek companies did not try to imitate or copy the trademark used by the Irish factory. That trademark has remained essentially the same with slight variations since the early 1860s. The mark incorporates a wolfhound, a harp, tower, and shamrocks with a banner containing the word "BELLEEK." No American Belleek mark remotely resembled that trademark, except for the word "Belleek." The American companies were not trying to trick Americans into thinking that their porcelain was made in Ireland. In fact, Ott & Brewer used "Trenton" and "N.J." in one of their Belleek marks. The early American Belleek manufacturers wanted above all to prove that quality porcelain could be made in America as well as in Europe. They were ultimately successful in that goal because the porcelain made by those several companies during the American Belleek era is still considered to be the finest work of the American porcelain industry and ranks on par with European porcelain made during the same time.

The American Belleek era was relatively short-lived, lasting only from 1883 until about 1930--less than fifty years. The total number of companies involved in making American Belleek was fewer than twenty during that time, including firms in both Trenton, N.J., and Ohio. Most of the companies were in business for only a few years. In fact, only five were in operation for more than ten years, and only one, Lenox, Inc., is in business today.

Two major factors brought about the downfall of the companies and the end of what can be called the American Belleek era. First and foremost was the economic factor. The porcelain was expensive to produce and thus expensive to purchase. The financial crisis in the United States during the 1890s took its toll on some of the earlier companies. The stock market crash of 1929 and the beginning of the Depression in 1930 adversely affected the later firms. During hard times of any period, there is not the demand for expensive items, and American Belleek porcelain would have been classified as such. The companies were also constantly in competition with imported foreign porcelain throughout the entire period of American Belleek manufacture. Because of such obstacles, the companies eventually had either to close or to change production to making more utilitarian and less expensive products.

The second and ultimate reason for the end of the American Belleek era occurred in 1929. At that time, the Irish Belleek Pottery Limited was successful in a suit filed against the Morgan Belleek China Company of Canton, Ohio. The court ruled that the Irish firm had the exclusive right to the name "Belleek" (Degenhardt, 1978). That ruling thus made it illegal for any American pottery to mark or market porcelain as "Belleek."

Therefore, after 1930, the American Belleek era was effectively over. Either the firms producing that type of porcelain were already out of business by that time, or those still in business stopped using "Belleek" to identify their products. New companies making a Belleek-type porcelain also had to refrain from using "Belleek" to advertise their products. Without that identifying term, there was really little to distinguish American Belleek porcelain made during the 1920s to 1930 from some other American porcelain made after 1930. One example is the Castleton China Company of New Castle, Pennsylvania, which began producing porcelain about 1940 (Lehner, 1980). Castleton porcelain had a parian body and a lustrous glaze (Gatchell, 1944). The Castleton porcelain, however, was not called "Belleek," but the quality of the porcelain and its method of manufacture were similar to porcelain made by American dinnerware companies during the 1920s which was marked and advertised as "Belleek" porcelain.

American porcelain made after 1930, even if it was a Belleek-type body composition, is considered totally on its own merits, and not as an example of American Belleek. Such porcelain is collected as a separate category of china according to the maker's name. The Lenox company is a good example to illustrate this point. When I was photographing for this book, dealers and collectors would ask if I wanted examples of Lenox or Lenox Belleek. Lenox porcelain made after 1930 is quite collectible of course. The body of the firm's porcelain did not change after 1930, but the word "Belleek" is not associated with Lenox porcelain after that time, because the word "Belleek" was no longer used in the marks or marketing of the company's porcelain. (In fact Lenox discontinued the use of the word "Belleek" in its porcelain marks about 1924; see the Lenox, Inc., entry in the photograph section for elaboration.)

For collectors, decorative and artistic items are usually more desirable than tableware or place settings. After 1930, American china manufacturers concentrated almost totally on dinnerware production. Very little in the line of art porcelain was made by American companies during and after the Depression years. In fact most American Belleek art objects were made before 1910. Thus, the year 1930 can be used as a rather precise cut-off date marking the end of the American Belleek era.

Collecting American Belleek

For the short history of the American Belleek era, the output of the several companies was quite prolific. Because a large variety of items was manufactured over a limited length of time, American Belleek is a very desirable collecting category. The age of the porcelain qualifies American Belleek as a real collectible. Examples are at least fifty years old, and many are close to one hundred years old.

A recent dimension has been added to American Belleek's collectibility because of the increasing awareness and demand for "Americana" of all types--from furniture to glass to pottery. American porcelain is not so plentiful as many other fields of Americana; therefore, American Belleek porcelain occupies a unique place in that realm of collecting. Today, interest in American Belleek is not confined only to porcelain collectors.

American companies, which from circa 1883 to 1930, manufactured porcelain identified as "Belleek" are presented in alphabetical order in the next major part of this book. Pertinent historical information, marks, and photographs are included for each company. Three general topics concerning American Belleek are discussed here: marks which identify American Belleek; the decoration on American Belleek; and the availability and prices of American Belleek.

Identifying Marks

The most important method of identifying American Belleek is by the manufacturer's trademark. Although American Belleek companies copied the Irish Belleek porcelain in method of manufacture, design, and decoration during the early years, resemblance to the Irish Belleek is really not the chief means of knowing whether a piece of porcelain is an example of American Belleek. Except for the distinguishing name "Belleek" in the mark, there is often little visible to the naked eye that looks like the Irish porcelain. We can tell if the object is porcelain by holding it up to a light and seeing if the piece is translucent rather than opaque, but we cannot easily differentiate a hard-paste porcelain body from a Belleek or bone-china porcelain body. Moreover, a wide range of decoration can be found on American Belleek, and many decoration themes were very much like those used on European hard-paste porcelain made during the same time. Although the American companies often decorated similarly to each other, there were also styles and decorative themes unique to each company. But manufacturer's marks are the basic way to identify one American company's Belleek porcelain from another.

For collectors, it is indeed fortunate that the American firms marked most of their porcelain. Exact dates when certain marks were used are not always clear or precise, but the specific company that made a particular piece usually can be identified. Because most of the companies were in business for a limited time, the exact date when a specific mark was used is not nearly so important as it is when companies have longer histories. Only two firms made American Belleek for more than twenty years. Willets and Lenox each made this type of porcelain over a span of twenty-four years, still not a very long period.

Fourteen American Belleek companies are discussed in this book. Ten of those used the word "Belleek" in at least one of their marks. Some of those ten also had other marks on Belleek porcelain which did not include the word "Belleek." Therefore it is important for collectors to recognize and be aware of the marks used by the different companies. Each manufacturer's marks are described and illustrated later in the book. Some of those made other types of pottery in addition to Belleek porcelain. Only the marks used on Belleek ware are shown here, not all of the various marks that a company may have used during its history. The dates of companies and marks refer to the firms' periods of manufacturing Belleek which may or may not coincide with the founding and closing dates of each company.

Three of the fourteen American Belleek manufacturers changed the spelling of Belleek by substituting a single "L" for the double "L," making the word "Beleek." Information about those three companies is very scant. Perlee, Inc. (Trenton Beleek), and the American Beleek Company, Inc., were both Trenton, New Jersey, firms that spelled the word with a single "L." Lehner (1980) shows that Perlee was listed in the Trenton City Directories from 1926 to 1930 and that the American Beleek Company was listed only in the 1954 Trenton directory. Lehner (1983) also notes that a company in Fredricksburg, Ohio, used the "Beleek" spelling. She does not give the name of that company or comment on its production, except to say that the company was in business for only one year (1954). I show two examples and the mark for the Trenton American Beleek Company, Inc. The mark shown for that company is quite fuzzy and therefore not easy to read. Enlargement of the transparency, however, made the writing legible enough for me to describe the mark in its caption. Two examples and the mark are also shown for pieces just marked "Beleek" without any company name, initial, or logo. It is possible those pieces could have been made by the

Fredricksburg, Ohio, company. The porcelain with that mark and the pieces with the American Beleek Company, Inc., mark, however do not appear to have been made as late as 1954.

In the Time-Life (1980, Volume B) article on American Belleek porcelain, Perlee, the American Beleek Company, and the Bellmark Pottery are said to have made lesser quality Belleek in the 1940s and 1950s. The article, however, inexplicably shows the dates for Perlee as 1922 to 1930. Other information (see the Perlee, Inc. entry in the photography section) supports the 1920s to 1930 period for that company rather than the 1940s and 1950s. The Bellmark Pottery was founded in 1893 in Trenton to make druggists' and plumbers' supplies (Barber, 1904). No other references state that Bellmark made Belleek porcelain. The Time-Life photographs identify an undecorated mug with an embossed figure on the front as an example of Bellmark Belleek; the mark on that piece is not described or illustrated to show if either "Belleek" or "Beleek" was part of the mark.

Because few examples are found with the "Beleek" spelling, it is difficult to glean much information about this particular area of American Belleek. It seems reasonable that companies reverted to spelling the word with only one "L" after the Irish Belleek Pottery Limited started legal proceedings against the Morgan Belleek China Company. Perhaps the companies thought they legally could circumvent the problem or the ultimate court's decision by changing the spelling of the word. Maybe more examples and information will surface to clarify the histories of those companies.

The fourteenth company included in this book did not mark its porcelain with either "Belleek," or "Beleek." That firm was Knowles, Taylor & Knowles of East Liverpool, Ohio. "Lotus Ware" was the name given to KTK's porcelain. Because of the particular history of the company and the nature of its porcelain (see the section on Knowles, Taylor & Knowles for elaboration), many collectors consider Lotus Ware an integral part of the American Belleek production. Other American porcelain made during the same time period (ca. 1883 to 1930), even if it was a Belleek-type, is not considered American Belleek if "Belleek" was not used in the marks of those firms' products.

Questionable Manufacturers

A few isolated examples and references indicate that some other companies, in addition to the ones I list in this book, made Belleek porcelain. I have not included those four companies because one of them (Delaware Pottery) only experimented with the Belleek technique. Two others (Bellmark and Glasgow) are mentioned in only one reference and no information indicated that the two companies did in fact mark their wares as Belleek. The fourth company (Sterling) marked its ware "Belleek," but the product was not really "Belleek." It is pertinent to draw attention to those several names, however. Readers might wonder why the companies are not presented here if they have seen them mentioned elsewhere as American Belleek manufacturers.

The Delaware Pottery of Trenton, New Jersey, did manufacture some Belleek porcelain. Barber (1893) says that the company was founded in 1884 to make industrial china, but that one of the partners of the company, Thomas Connelly, experimented with making Belleek about 1886. Connelly had previously been associated with the Irish Belleek works. Connelly died in 1890, and the Delaware Pottery never developed Belleek production on a commercial basis. Barber does not say if the firm marked the examples with "Belleek" or not. It is unlikely that any examples survived. (If a reader has an example, please send a picture of the piece and the mark!)

The Bellmark Pottery discussed earlier is not included. Time-Life (Volume B, 1980) was the only reference which noted the company as a Belleek manufacturer. An example was shown, but no marks or specific dates were given for the company.

The Official 1983 Guide to Pottery & Porcelain (Hudgeons, 1983; pp. 28, 61) states that the Glasgow Pottery manufactured American Belleek. The company is used as an example of an American Belleek company under the entry for "Belleek" in the book's glossary. The Glasgow Pottery was founded in Trenton, New Jersey in 1893. The company made a wide variety of ceramic products including granite ware, majolica, stone china, decorated ware, vitrified china, and hotel and steamboat china (Barber, 1904). Hudgeons' book is the only one that I found, however, that said the company made Belleek. That information is not even given in the earlier (1980) edition of the book authored by Robinson and Feeny. Moreover, the information under the Glasgow Pottery entry in the revised edition's section of factories has not been revised to indicate that the company made Belleek porcelain. "Belleek" is not shown in any marks of the company. Thus, whether the Glasgow Pottery identified any of its production as "Belleek" remains unclear.

Although the word "Belleek" or "Beleek" in a mark is the key for identifying American Belleek, there is one exception to that rule of thumb. One company marked earthenware items with a "Belleek" mark. The mark is just "STERLING" over "BELLEEK." The ware is decorated with sterling silver designs. Some collectors think the origin of the pieces may be either England or Ohio. A "Sterling" pottery was located in both places. The mark could be a double play on words designating the company name and type of decoration (unless some pieces--and I have seen none--were decorated without silver). Obviously, the "Belleek" name was intended to "cash in" on either the Irish or American Belleek market. (In the same way, companies in both England and America marked earthenware "Limoges" to take advantage of the Limoges, France, porcelain market during the same time period as the American Belleek era.) Although "Belleek" is part of the mark, and even though the Irish Belleek Pottery marked their earthenware as well as their porcelain "Belleek," the word has come to define a special type of porcelain. Thus, American or English earthenware examples marked "Belleek" are not actually considered to be "Belleek." Such objects may be of novel interest to American Belleek collectors, however.

Unmarked Belleek

Occasionally American Belleek manufacturers did not mark their porcelain, and as a result, there are examples of unmarked American Belleek. Some items were not marked through oversight in the production process. Articles may not have been marked if they did not meet company quality standards, and objects such as buttonhooks and hand mirrors were difficult to mark. Often all of the pieces in a set of china did not receive a mark. Unmarked porcelain cannot always be attributed as the product of a specific company or identified as American Belleek rather than as porcelain made by another American or European factory. In some cases, however, company advertisements, catalogs, or brochures supply evidence that certain items were made by a company. Frequently, marked pieces can also be found which are identical to an unmarked specimen. Beginning collectors may be hesitant to purchase unmarked objects while advanced collectors have the necessary expertise and eye for identifying unmarked American Belleek and purchase such items without a second thought. Scarce and unusual items that were probably never marked are in fact very desirable and quite expensive, whereas the more common types of items are usually a good bit lower in price if they are not factory marked.

American Belleek Decoration

A variety of decorative themes, finishes, and trims enhance American Belleek. Irridescent lusters, matte or satin finishes, beaded or jewelled designs, gold paste decor, enamelling, sponged gold and dry brush work are some of the techniques that were employed by several of the American Belleek factories. All American Belleek, however, was not decorated at the factory.

Most of the American Belleek companies were in business when painting on porcelain was popular as a hobby for young ladies or as a special professional pursuit or occupation. Undecorated porcelain known as "blanks" or "white ware" was imported from Europe for American china painters during the late Victorian era through the early part of the twentieth century. The American Belleek companies operating during that time also took advantage of that special market by selling undecorated porcelain as well as factory decorated items.

For collectors, it is not always easy to tell whether a particular piece was decorated at the factory or not. The companies either did not mark their white ware differently from their decorated ware, of if they did initiate such a practice, they were usually not consistent in its use. Because most American Belleek has handpainted decoration rather than transfer designs, the decoration cannot always be the clue as to whether or not a piece was decorated at the factory. American Belleek exhibiting the lusters, finishes, trims, etc., mentioned above can in most cases safely be identified as factory decorated. Totally handpainted pieces with floral, fruit, and portrait themes, for example, leave more room for doubt unless the object is signed by an artist who has been identified as having worked for one or more of the American Belleek manufacturers. Some of those factory artists are known, but by no means all of them. Moreover, the majority of factory decorated American Belleek is not signed. A signature on a piece of American Belleek does not automatically mean that the piece was factory decorated. Amateur artists especially liked to sign their work, and probably more "signed" pieces found today were handpainted by amateur artists than by factory or professional artists. The type of signature as well as the quality of the art work can often be used to differentiate amateur art from professional decoration. Bold signatures written across the face of an object or on the back or base of an item, sometimes including a date and perhaps even an occasion, indicate a non-professional artist. Professional artists either initial or write their name unobtrusively on the face of their work. Certain factories did have their artists initial the backs of pieces rather than the face, but the signature as well as the art work are usually easily distinguishable from the amateur's.

Professional decorating studios, silver companies, and jewelry stores which decorated white ware with handpainted designs, silver overlay, or gilding and monogramming frequently added their own mark to the porcelain manufacturer's mark. The origin of that type of decoration is relatively easy to determine. Unsigned handpainted American Belleek is usually the most difficult to decide whether or not the decoration was applied at the factory. All amateur artists did not sign their work and neither did all factory or professional artists. In most instances, blatantly amateur decoration can be separated from quality decoration. Quality decoration usually complicates the problem of making a precise decision regarding factory or non-factory decoration.

Collectors recognize factory decorated and non-factory decorated as two distinct categories of American Belleek. Pieces known to be factory decorated are the most coveted, but non-factory decorated American Belleek also is collected because such pieces are examples of various manufacturer's products. They have a "Belleek" mark, and were made during the American Belleek era. Non-factory decoration of a professional quality ranks only somewhat lower on the collectibility scale. Certain examples decorated by art studios such as Pickard may in fact be more expensive than factory decorated American Belleek. Non-professional or obviously amateur decoration does not mean that a piece is not worth collecting. The item may represent a unique type of object, or it may be one made by a firm that was in business for such a short time that any example from that company, however decorated, is highly desirable. Certain amateur decorated pieces may also fit in well with one's collection. The "Belleek" mark, however, is usually the overriding factor for collecting non-professionally decorated American Belleek.

In the photographs of American Belleek featured in this book, items are factory decorated unless otherwise indicated. The term "Professional Decoration" is used to describe quality decoration by either a professional decorating studio or an artist whose workmanship appears professional. "Non-professional Decoration" implies amateur china painting.

Availability and Prices

There is not as much American Belleek porcelain available as there is European porcelain of the same vintage. Although American Belleek is prized for its artistic qualities, its relative scarcity also contributes substantially to its collectibility today. American Belleek collectors are scattered throughout the United States, but access to American Belleek is still centered around the areas where it was made--namely in the Eastern region of the United States. Finding American Belleek at antique shops or estate sales in the midwestern, southern, and western states is not easy. In fact, I have come across many dealers (selling china) who do not know what "American Belleek" is. American Belleek collectors, wherever they are located, must be particularly diligent in their search. That fact does not seem to hinder, but only to peak, collectors' interest!

Factory decorated American Belleek commands the highest prices overall, especially the porcelain made by the earlier companies such as Ott & Brewer, Willets, the American Art China Company, the Ceramic Art Company, the Columbian Art Pottery Company, and Knowles, Taylor & Knowles. Examples from the Coxon and Morgan companies, which appear much later, are also quite expensive because of their scarcity. A factory artist's signature, unusual body design, richness of decoration, and even the size of an object (such as miniatures or floor vases) add value to certain American Belleek articles.

More non-factory decorated American Belleek appears to be available than factory decorated items. Non-factory decorated pieces which exhibit quality art work are very close in price to factory decorated ware. Poorly handpainted items are often priced much lower than factory or professionally decorated pieces, and they should be, for it is the beauty of the decoration which contributes to the collectible nature of the porcelain.

Undecorated American Belleek is sometimes overlooked by collectors. There is not a large amount of undecorated American Belleek available. A few pieces do exist which for some reason were never decorated by the factory or individuals. Undecorated pieces can be very attractive, especially if they have an unusual shape or applied work. Currently prices for the undecorated ware are much lower than prices for even the most amateur decorated American Belleek. Collectors might be on the alert for undecorated examples.

Overall prices for most American Belleek range from expensive to very expensive. Prices are probably higher on average in the eastern part of the United States because, historically, the concentration of the porcelain has been in that region. For some other categories of antiques or collectibles, where the supply is centered in the East, the price escalates the farther west the item travels, but that is not necessarily true concerning American Belleek. Lack of knowledge about this area of collecting would account for the lower prices in other regions. For the serious and dedicated collector, "good buys" can still be found, especially pieces made by Willets and Lenox, and even occasionally Coxon and Gordon items. On the other hand, because examples of any firm's American Belleek are not too plentiful in some parts of the U.S., very mediocre examples in those regions may have a very high price tag.

Information for the Price Guide for American Belleek illustrated in this book was derived from a variety of sources including items for sale by shops, shows, and collectors. All examples were currently owned by collectors or dealers. No photographs were taken of pieces in museums; some of the items shown are like those in museums, and several are in fact so unique and rare, that perhaps they should be in museums. Being in a museum, however, does not mean that an item is "priceless." It is difficult to assign prices to certain examples. In some instances for the American Belleek presented here, there was no current price information. Some pieces had been purchased by the collectors years ago. The prices paid at an earlier time would not reflect accurately the prices those items might bring on today's market. A price range was compiled by taking into account current prices for other American Belleek which were available plus weighing additional factors for each piece such as rarity, uniqueness, age, and art work.

A wide variety of American Belleek is presented in the following company and photograph section of this book. Factory decorated, professionally decorated and amateur non-factory decorated American Belleek are illustrated. Various kinds of applied work, different body finishes, a broad range of decorative themes, and many types of items have been included. Readers may not find "exact" examples to match pieces they may own or buy. That should be expected because so many pieces were manufactured, and much was hand decorated. Thus many examples are one-of-a-kind. By comparing manufacturer, type of object, and method and subject of decoration, price ranges for many other examples of American Belleek can be known.

Prices quoted here are for items in mint condition. Please note that the term "rare" is used in only a very few instances to describe certain items although many examples are perhaps quite scarce. A multitude of factors influence final purchasing price of any antique or collectible. The pricing information presented for American Belleek is intended to be used only as guide. It is not intended to set prices.

Companies, Marks,
and
Photographs

American Art China Works (AAC)

The American Art China Works was founded in 1891 by Rittenhouse and Evans in Trenton, New Jersey. Their aim was to produce high quality American porcelain with the emphasis on "American Made." Fine quality American Belleek porcelain was made in tableware and art objects.

The company used two different marks on its porcelain. Mark 1 incorporates the owners' initials. Because of this mark, the company is often referred to by collectors as "Rittenhouse and Evans" rather than by the firm name. Mark 2 is composed of the company initials and "BELLEEK CHINA." Note that the word "Belleek" is not a part of Mark 1.

The American Art China company sold both decorated and undecorated porcelain. The examples shown here appear to have been professionally decorated. The marks do not distinguish white ware from decorated ware, however. The Napoleon Jug could very well have been decorated outside the factory. The roses on the creamer in Plate 4 may also have been added after the piece left the factory. Because the company was in business for only about four years, until ca. 1895 (Time-Life, Volume B, 1978), any example is in demand.

American Art China Mark 1 with Owners' initials (Rittenhouse and Evans) in blue, ca. 1891 to 1895.

American Art China Mark 2 with company initials and "BELLEEK CHINA" in blue, ca. 1891 to 1895.

PLATE 1. AAC Mark 2. Vases, matched pair, 12″h, large pastel colored flowers on white body, pale yellow finish on neck, gilded embossed designs on handles, gold trim.

PLATE 2. AAC Mark 1. Individual Salt, 2½″h, pink interior, sponged gold work on scalloped border and base.

PLATE 3. AAC Mark 2. Small Bowl, 2½″h, 5″d, scalloped border, dainty pink and white floral decoration inside and out.

PLATE 4. AAC Mark 2. Open Sugar and Creamer, not a matched pair. Sugar, 2¼″h, pink interior, crimped border with sponged gold trim, handpainted flowers on exterior. Creamer, 4″h, sponged gold trim inside fancy shaped border, handpainted floral border around outer center, gold trim.

PLATE 5. AAC Mark 1. Creamer, 3½″h, soft pink interior, gold trim.

PLATE 6. The Mark on the base of this pitcher is printed "Patent Applied For, Alfred M. Evans." Napoleon jug, 4″h, handpainted.

American Beleek Company, Inc. (ABC)

Specific dating information is not available for this company. Lehner (1980) found that the company was listed in the Trenton, New Jersey, Directories in 1954. The mark on examples is a globe with "American Beleek Company, Inc." That mark is not very distinct on pieces seen. The quality of the porcelain is good, but few examples are available.

American Beleek Company, Inc., Mark. Full company name printed in banner around a globe, date uncertain.

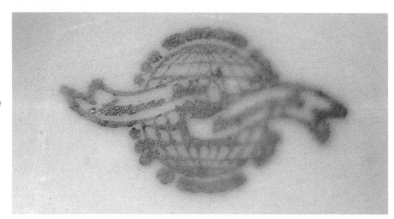

PLATE 7. ABC Mark. Shell, 4″x5″, pink luster interior.

PLATE 8. ABC Mark. Swan, 4″h, 4½″l, gold trim.

Beleek

No specific company has been identified which marked its porcelain with only the word "Beleek." The mark appears on the items illustrated in red or green. The quality of the porcelain is good. The cup may not have been decorated at the factory, and perhaps the green mark was used to designate the company's white ware line. The pitcher resembles early American Belleek in form. The mark on the pitcher is in red, possibly indicative of factory decoration. Examples are scarce.

Beleek Mark (in green or red), date unknown.

PLATE 9. "Beleek" mark in red on base. Ewer, branch-style handle in brown tones, handpainted roses on body.

PLATE 10. "Beleek" mark in green. Demi-tasse Cup, 2¼"h, gold decor, fine quality porcelain. Item is probably not factory decorated.

The Ceramic Art Company (CAC)

Jonathan Coxon, Sr., and Walter Scott Lenox founded the Ceramic Art Company in 1889 in Trenton, New Jersey. Both men had previously worked for Ott and Brewer, and thus had knowledge and experience in the manufacturing and decorating process for Belleek porcelain.

The firm used several different marks. The word "Belleek," however, is found on only one of those marks (see Mark 1). Barber (1893) states that the mark was used for undecorated porcelain, and that the mark was printed in different colors. Examples with Mark 1, however, often do exhibit factory decoration.

Mark 2 contains the full name of the company printed inside a large wreath shape. This mark was used on special orders commissioned by groups or individuals and is not frequently seen.

The company initials "CAC" printed inside a wreath is a third mark. This mark is similar to Mark 4 except Mark 4 has "Lenox" printed underneath the wreath. Mark 4 is known as the "transition" mark of the company; this indicates the period (1896-1906) after Jonathan Coxon, Sr., left the company and before Walter Lenox incorporated the firm under the Lenox name. Robinson and Feeny (1980) assume, and it seems reasonable, that Mark 3 (without the "Lenox" name) was in use prior to Mark 4. Items with one of those two marks are usually factory decorated.

It is not possible to place an exact date or time period for Marks 1, 2, and 3, except that they were first used after 1889. There is no consensus on when each was discontinued, before 1906. There is also no agreement concerning the purpose of the different colors of those marks or the dates when different colored marks were introduced or discontinued. Because the entire time span for using those marks was only about seventeen years, the specific dates and the colors of the marks should not command excessive attention. The type and quality of decoration are the basic criteria to determine whether an item was or was not decorated at the factory.

Several artists worked for the Ceramic Art Company during the seventeen-year period. Robinson and Feeny (1980, p.81) identify Boullemier, Campana, Clayton, DeLan, Geyer, Heidrich, Kuhn, Laurence, Marsh, Martell, George Morley, William Morley, Nosek, Sully, Swalk, Wirkner, and Witte as CAC artists who may have signed their handpainted decoration. From that large number of names, it seems that quite a few pieces would have a factory artist's signature. It is apparent from currently available items, however, that the majority of factory-decorated CAC items were not artist signed. Display pieces such as vases, pitchers, or plates decorated with portrait or floral themes are the pieces most often seen with a CAC factory artist's signature. Signed examples command a higher price.

CAC MARK 1. "Belleek" Palette Mark in red, lavender, brown, green, or black, after 1889 and before 1906.

CAC MARK 2. "The Ceramic Art Co., Trenton, N.J." in lavender or green, after 1889 and before 1906.

CAC MARK 3. "CAC" initials in Wreath in lavender, green, or brown, after 1889 and probably before 1896.

CAC MARK 4. "CAC" initials in Wreath with "Lenox" printed underneath, lavender, green, gold, 1896-1906.

PLATE 11. CAC Mark 4 in green. Vase, 15″h, handpainted portrait on rich maroon background with detailed beaded gold frame, gold floral designs, and turquoise beading at neck and base, artist signed "Nosek," noted factory artist.

PLATE 12. CAC Mark 3 in lavender for Bell on left, 4½″h. (See Columbian Art Pottery for description and price of bell on right.) Delft-type decoration of lighthouse.

PLATE 13. Bell, unmarked, but attributed to CAC, tulip shaped, silver decor.

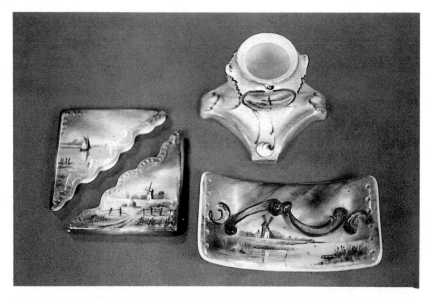

PLATE 14. CAC Mark 4 in lavender. Desk Set, decorated in Delft style. Inkwell is the only piece marked. Inkwell, 6″h, lid missing; Pair of Blotter Corners, 5″x4″; Blotter, 6″l.

PLATE 15. CAC Mark 3 in lavender. Covered Trinket Box, 5¼″l, scenic decor in Delft style, embossed scroll designs trimmed in gold, artist signed "MM."

PLATE 16. CAC Mark 1 in lavender. Demi-tasse Cups, 2″h, called "Engagement" shape because of ring-styled handles. Gold paste floral designs inside cups, outside undecorated except for gold trim on base and handles.

PLATE 17. CAC Mark 4 in lavender. Individual Salt Dip and Pepper Shaker, mixed floral decor, gold trim. Pepper Shaker is unmarked because of hole for cork in base.

PLATE 18. CAC Mark 3 in green. Miniature Mugs, "Mauser" sterling silver overlay, professional decoration: 2½″h, 2″h, 2¼″h. Mug on left has "Boston" written on front, the one on the right has a shield with the date "1903." These two are the same form while the center mug is barrel shaped and decorated in a coral rather than brown glaze. Miniatures are highly sought by collectors.

PLATE 19. CAC Mark 1 in green. Miniature Vase, 3¾″h, purple luster on body, neck undecorated.

PLATE 20. CAC Mark 1 in lavender. Loving Cup, 8½″h, figural child's head forms top of handles. This type of handpainted monk decor in browntones is noted by Barber (1901, p.488) as an interesting theme of decoration used by the company. Barber shows the same mold but with a different decoration subject in his discussion.

PLATE 21. CAC Mark 1 in lavender. Loving Cup, 8½″h, 3 ornate handles with molded child's head at top of each, handpainted violet decor.

PLATE 22. CAC Mark 1 in red. Chocolate Pot, 11″h, bark finish, gold paste floral designs with lavender leaves in background on matte body, twig-shaped handle and finial, note slanted lid position.

PLATE 23. CAC Mark 1 in brown. Chocolate Pot, 12″h, Mermaid molded spout and handle, embossed fish on lower part and on lid, handpainted marine life, gold trim.

PLATE 24. CAC Mark 1 in lavender. Vase, 22″h, handpainted multicolored chrysanthemums, ornate handles, pedestal footed base.

PLATE 25. CAC Mark 1 in lavender. Vase, 18″h, handpainted lavender and white flowers, professional decoration.

PLATE 26. CAC Mark 1 in green. Vase, 22″h, hand-painted herons with a different view on three sides, stylized gold borders outline the three sides as iris leaves with flower in gold on black background at top of vase. This example is not factory decorated but quite detailed. The vase is a particularly large one.

PLATE 27. The second side of the "Heron" vase.
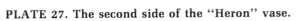

PLATE 28. The third side of the "Heron" vase.

PLATE 29. CAC Mark 1 in red and green. Miniature Oil Lamps, known in Victorian times as "Sparking" lamps for young lovers, 2¼"h. The one on the left was factory decorated, and the CAC Mark is in red; the one on the right has the CAC Mark 1 in green and it was not factory decorated. Note the lamp on the right also has the tiny brass snuffer to extinguish the lamp. "Sparking Lamps" are rare items.

PLATE 30. Table lamp, 20½"h, unmarked, but attributed to CAC. Undecorated, graceful shape with embossed designs on lightly scalloped base.

PLATE 31. CAC Mark 1 in lavender. Inkwell, 4½"h, handpainted chrysanthemums, gold trim, not factory decorated.

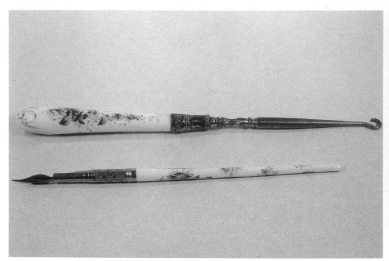

PLATE 32. Pen, 9″l; Buttonhook, 7¾″l, unmarked but attributed to CAC, factory decorated with multicolored floral designs, gold trim. See following photograph for similar decoration. These types of items are rare.

PLATE 33. CAC Mark 1 in lavender with "For Davis Collamore & Co., New York," (noted retail establishment). Dresser Items: Hairbrush, 9½″l; Hand Mirror, 7¾″l; Holder or base for Nail Buffer (Buffer part is missing), 6″l. Multicolored floral designs, gold trim on embossed scroll designs on body, rare items.

PLATE 34. CAC Mark 1 in lavender. Clock, 9″h, footed, fancy rococo shape, ring type finial, handpainted floral decor with gold trim and blue beading. The clock has Ansonia works, rare item.

PLATE 35. CAC Mark 1 in lavender. Vase, 22½″h, extensively applied gold scroll designs overlaying handpainted violet flowers on cream background. Professional handpainting, gold work appears added. Very large vase.

PLATE 36. CAC Mark 1 in green. Vase, 12¼″h, mixed floral decor on bottom half on light lavender background. Gold enamelled scroll and floral designs on undecorated body on top half, professional decoration.

PLATE 37. CAC Mark 4 in green. Cream Soup Cup, 2″h; Saucer, 5½″d, Irish style "Tridacna" body form, gold trim.

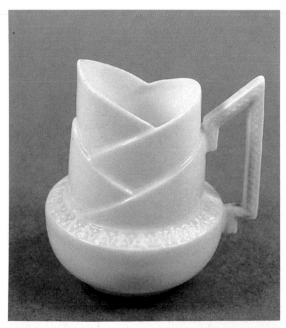

PLATE 38. Mark 1 in brown. Pitcher, 3¾″h, whiteware, wrap-around shaped upper body, embossed work on bottom part and on angular-shaped handle.

PLATE 39. Mark 4 in green. Sauce Bowl, 2½″h, 5″d, decorated with gold lines and pink floral sprays in two-handled sterling silver holder, 7″d, marked "J.E. Caldwell."

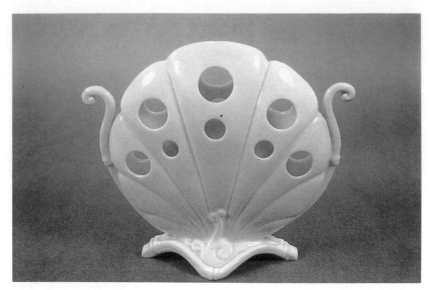

PLATE 40. CAC Mark 1 in brown. Vase, 6″h, 7″w, shell form with large circular openings on each side, snail-shaped handles and embossed design on four-footed base, undecorated.

PLATE 41. CAC Mark 1 in brown. Planter, 7½″h, crimped border decorated with gold on interior side of ruffles, stylized lavender flowers with green leaves on white background, gold trim on double-looped designs around opening, Art Nouveau style handle.

PLATE 42. CAC Mark 1 in lavender. Planter, same shape as planter in preceding photograph. This piece exhibits the unique decoration of Kate Sears, a noted CAC factory sculptor, who carved designs with a jackknife on the clay body of the porcelain before it was fired. This piece features a lamb and shepherd, pink finish on interior, gilded handle. Kate Sears' work is quite rare.

PLATE 43. CAC Mark 1 in lavender. Vase, 6½″h, "Cabbage" or "Lotus" leaf shape, gold paste floral decor on dark green and brown background, yellow luster interior, crimped border at top, three-footed base wth open work forming stems and buds.

PLATE 44. Unmarked, attributed to CAC. Tankard, 13″h, handpainted figural and scenic decor, artist signed "Heidrich" (CAC factory artist).

PLATE 45. CAC Mark 1 in brown. Double-Spouted Pitcher, 3″h, violet flowers on white background, cream finish on spouts, gold trim.

PLATE 46. Another view of Double-Spouted Pitcher.

PLATE 47. CAC Mark 1 in lavender. Vase, 11″h, gold paste floral decor on matte finish, circular branch-style handles.

PLATE 48. CAC Mark 1 in lavender. Ewer, 7½"h, gold paste floral designs, creamy matte finish on body, pink finish on neck.

PLATE 49. CAC Mark 1 in lavender. Pitcher, 4"h, ribbed and embossed body designs, scattered pink flowers, spattered gold work on base.

PLATE 50. CAC Mark 1 in lavender. Plate, 7½"d, luster finish, shading from pale pink to green, gold trim on scalloped border, signed "MJB 1901." The signature designates that the gold trim was not applied at the factory.

PLATE 51. CAC Mark 1 in lavender, Candy or Nut Bowl, 2″h, 6¼″l, jagged border with curled handle, footed, pink interior finish, gold trim, artist signed "BWE" in gold, professional decoration.

PLATE 52. CAC Mark 1 in lavender. Swan Individual Salt, 1¾″h, gilded trim; Spoon, 3″l, undecorated, rare item.

PLATE 53. CAC Mark 3 in brown. Stein, 7½″h, handpainted monk with wine casks, browntones, Art Nouveau design in silver on top of lid.

PLATE 54. CAC Mark 1 in green. Mug, 6″h, handpainted apples on orange background, not factory decorated.

PLATE 55. CAC Mark 1 in green. Stein, 8″h, desert and sunset decoration, not factory decorated.

PLATE 56. CAC Mark 1 in green. Mug, 5½″h, hand-painted stylized tulips handpainted in gold and outlined in red, black background, not factory decorated.

PLATE 57. CAC Mark 3 in brown. Pharmacy Jug, 4½″h, glossy brown glaze, "Rx" in sterling silver overlay on front, sterling silver lid, professional decoration.

PLATE 58. CAC Mark 1 in brown. Vase, 10¼″h, large white flowers outlined in pink and large pink flowers outlined in gold with gold paste leaf designs on creamy matte finish on lower part. Neck, extending to upper part of body, decorated with green floral designs on gold and green diamond-patterned background, outlined with raised gold border. Ornate neck design fashioned in four sections with gilded interior.

PLATE 59. CAC Mark 1 in lavender. Demi-tasse liner decorated with pastel and gold paste floral designs on interior and exterior, sterling silver holder.

PLATE 60. CAC Mark 1 in brown with "Berlin" decorating studio mark. Ink Blotter Holder, 6"l, handpainted pink floral designs with butterflies, gold trim.

PLATE 61. CAC Mark 1 in lavender. Commemorative Item, Cup, 2½"h, Saucer, 4½"d, double portraits on cup with "See the Players Well Bestowed," small enamelled pink flowers on border.

PLATE 62. CAC Mark 2 in green. Commemorative Item, 5"h, "Anniversary Dinner of the Friendly Sons of Saint Patrick in the City of New York, Delmonicos, March 18, 1901."

PLATE 63. CAC Mark 1 in lavender. Vase, 10″h, ribbed neck, handpainted roses, gilded handles.

PLATE 64. CAC Mark 4 in lavender. Vase, 13¼"h, handpainted pink and white flowers on deep yellow to blue background, artist signed "Marsh," factory artist. "Glen-Iris" also appears with mark on base.

Columbian Art Pottery (CAP)

W.T. Morris and F.R. Willmore established the Columbian Art Pottery in Trenton, New Jersey, in 1893. The company was named in honor of the World's Columbian Exposition held in Chicago in 1893. References about this firm, however, are often made to the owners' names (Morris and Willmore) rather than the company name. This may confuse collectors because such listings without cross-references suggest that they were two separate American Belleek manufacturers.

Morris had previously worked at the Irish Belleek factory, and both Morris and Willmore had worked at the English Royal Worcester firm before coming to America. In Trenton, they both worked for Ott & Brewer before getting together and forming their own factory to produce American Belleek (Barber, 1893). The Columbian Art Pottery mark on Belleek porcelain was composed of a shield with the owners' initials. Souvenir and commemorative items, as well as artistic tableware, were made. The company was in business until about 1902 (Lehner, 1980).

Columbian Art Pottery Mark (CAP) in black, blue, red, ca. 1893 to 1902.

PLATE 65. CAP Mark in black. Mug, 5½"h, transfer design Monk decor in black tones.

PLATE 66. CAP Mark in black. Souvenir Tumbler, 4¼"h. Black and red lettering, "Souvenir David's Society, New York, 64th Annual Dinner, Sherry's, March 1, 1899."

PLATE 67. CAP Mark in blue. Liberty Bell, 4½″h, blue transfer design of Independence Hall. Printed inscription around top of bell, "Proclaim Liberty Throughout All The Land Unto All The Inhabitants Thereon By Order of the Assembly of the Province of Pennsylvania For the State House in Phil. ADA." Inscription on the front under design, "Independence Hall 1776," and on the reverse side, "PASS AND STOW, PHILADA, MDCCLIII." This souvenir bell is highly sought by collectors.

PLATE 68. CAP Mark in red. Demi-tasse cup, 1½″h; Saucer, 4½″d, Irish "Tridacna" body pattern, gold trim originally on borders and handle.

PLATE 69. CAP Mark in red, Teapot, 7½″h, 9″l, unusual Dragon shape, gold paste leaf designs on cream-colored matte body finish with pinkish-brown highlights, gold trim. This design is very similar to the Irish Belleek "Chinese Tea Ware" (see Degenhardt, 1978, pp, 36 and 46). Rare design.

The Cook Pottery Company

The Cook Pottery Company was the successor to the Ott & Brewer firm in Trenton, New Jersey. The new company was established in 1894 with Charles Howell Cook as president. This factory manufactured earthenware as well as porcelain, and several different marks were used on the products. The most frequently found mark on the company's Belleek porcelain consisted of three feathers with "ETRURIA" printed in a ribbon shape underneath. "ETRURIA" referred to the original name of the pottery works founded in 1863 by Bloor, Ott, and Booth which became Ott & Brewer in 1865 (Barber, 1904).

The three-feather mark does not always have "Belleek" printed above the symbol. "Mellor & Co." or the initials "C.H.C." are sometimes found printed below the mark. Mellor referred to the Vice President of the company, F.G. Mellor, and C.H.C. are Cook's initials. Cook China Company closed about 1929 (Lehner, 1980), but the firm's Belleek production is not thought to have lasted very long after the company was established (Robinson and Feeny, 1980). The few examples of Cook Belleek available substantiates that hypothesis.

Cook Pottery Mark. Three feathers with "BELLEEK" printed above, "ETRURIA" and "C.H.C." printed below, in red, after 1894.

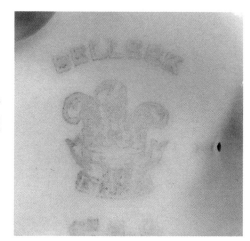

PLATE 70. Cook Mark, Individual Salt (on left), 1¾"h, 2½"d. (See Ott & Brewer for Salt on right.) Salt has three feet, handpainted leaf decor, gold trim.

Coxon Belleek Pottery

Frederick Coxon established Coxon Belleek Pottery in 1926 in Wooster, Ohio. His brother, Edward, and Edward's son, Edward, Jr., were also a part of the operation. Frederick and Edward's father was Jonathan Coxon. He had been a partner to Walter Lenox in The Ceramic Art Company established in Trenton, New Jersey, in 1889. Thus the brothers had access to the knowledge of making Belleek porcelain.

According to Heald (1959), the Coxons' venture was intended to compete with the Lenox firm, the successor to The Ceramic Art Company. The Coxons, however, faced competition closer to home by the Morgan Belleek China Company. This type of competition in luxury table porcelain plus the high cost of production and the beginning of the Depression forced the company to close in 1930 after only four years.

The quality of Coxon Belleek is considered to be as fine as any American Belleek. Dinnerware was the main line of the company. Coxon Belleek was sold across the country and was quite expensive for the times. Pieces were decorated with transfer designs, but these were filled in and retouched with handpainted work (Markham, 1962). Enamelling and coin-gold decoration were other characteristics of the porcelain. It is unlikely that any undecorated china was sold because the china painting era was just about over when the company was established. All examples shown are factory decorated. The china was marked with the name of the company.

Prices for Coxon Belleek are high today. Examples are scarce due to the short time of production. It should be noted that complete sets such as tea sets, dinner services, etc., would also command a higher price than individual pieces. Because of lack of knowledge, it is still sometimes possible to come across good buys in this china.

Coxon Belleek Mark in black, ca. 1926 to 1930.

PLATE 71. Coxon Mark, Dinner Plate, 10½″d, wide yellow outer border, inner border of tiny enamelled flowers, gold trim.

PLATE 72. Coxon Mark. Plate, 8″d, mixed floral decor, known as the "Bouquet" pattern.

PLATE 73. Coxon Mark, Tea Set, wide yellow outer border with blue and pink transfer floral designs, gold trim. Creamer, 5″h; Covered Sugar, 6″h; Teapot, 6½″h; Bread & Butter Plate, 6″d; Cup, 2″h, Saucer, 5″d.

Gordon Belleek

No company information was found for the firm that marked its products, "Gordon Belleek." It is possible that the company was located in Ohio. The examples seen are in the mode of later Lenox and Perlee Belleek of the late 1920s. Decoration is a mixture of transfer designs with handpainted work. The porcelain is of good quality.

Gordon Belleek Mark 1. Printed in black, dates unknown, probably circa late 1920s.

Gordon Belleek Mark 2. Printed in script fashion, in black.

PLATE 74. Gordon Belleek Mark 2. Plate, 7″d, peacocks and mixed floral decor, gold trim.

PLATE 75. Gordon Belleek Mark 1. Cup, 2½″h, Saucer, 5½″d, mixed floral decor on body and interior of cup.

Knowles, Taylor & Knowles China Company (KTK)

Knowles, Taylor & Knowles was incorporated in 1891 in East Liverpool, Ohio, but the origin of the company was much earlier. In 1854, Isaac W. Knowles and Isaac A. Harvey established a small pottery to make yellow ware. John N. Taylor and Homer S. Knowles joined Isaac Knowles in 1870 after Harvey left the company (making the owners Knowles, Taylor and Knowles). Joseph G. Lee and William A. Knowles became additional partners in 1888. All (except Harvey) formed the stock company under the name of the Knowles, Taylor & Knowles Company in 1891. Production was geared to white graniteware and hotel china (Barber, 1893).

Belleek-type porcelain was not made by the company until after 1887. At that time, Joshua Poole was hired from the Irish Belleek factory in order to teach and implement the Belleek technique (Schwartz, 1969). Porcelain production was halted, at least temporarily, in 1889 when a fire destroyed the factory. Although sources do not agree on the exact year, the company was able to make porcelain once more around 1890 or 1891. Examples were exhibited at the Chicago Exposition in 1893. The porcelain made after 1889 was not called ''Belleek'' even though it resembled the Irish Belleek body and glaze. The composition was not like that of the Irish Belleek, but was rather a bone china (Barber, 1893). Bone china used the calcined bones of animals in the preparation of the formula for the clay body paste. Knowles, Taylor & Knowles called this bone china, ''Lotus Ware.'' It is said that name was decided on because the first vase made was decorated with floral shapes designed after the Lotus blossom (Lehner, 1980).

Lotus Ware was definitely executed as an art porcelain. Graceful body shapes, often showing an Art Nouveau influence, intricate open work designs, and beautiful applied decoration of flowers, beading (jewelled), and filigree (fishnet) decor distinguished the porcelain. William and George Morley from England (later employed as artists for the Ceramic Art Company and Lenox, Inc.), and Henry Schmidt from Germany were decorators for the company. Henry Schmidt is particularly noted for his unique method of applied work to the porcelain body. Designs, made of a thick liquid paste composed of the same materials as the body of the porcelain, were ''squeezed'' from a container in desired forms onto the green ware (unbaked clay body) and then fired. Examples of Schmidt's work are highly sought. Note the various forms of his applied work on the examples in the photographs.

Although several different marks were used by the company on its products, only two were used on the Lotus Ware. One contained the company initials over ''China.'' The other included the initials with a star and crescent shape printed inside a circle with ''Lotus Ware'' printed underneath. A variation of that mark may have the company name written in full. Barber (1893) said that the KTK/CHINA mark was placed on white ware (the company sold undecorated as well as decorated porcelain), and that the Lotus Ware mark was used for factory decorated pieces. Examples prove, though, that the practice was not consistent. The Lily vase shown here in Plate 87 has the KTK/CHINA mark (see Mark 1). That mark contains some numbers and an initial. The initial probably refers to the decorator. Boger (1978) states that the factory decorated pieces included the artist's initial and the date. Some examples do have both initials and dates, but some factory decorated pieces do not, and we can see from the mark on the Lily vase, that there is only an initial and no date. The numbers would most likely refer to some inventory or product number.

Lotus Ware did not become the main production of Knowles, Taylor & Knowles. It was too expensive to manufacture. The economic situation in the United States during the early 1890s caused the company to terminate Lotus Ware production about 1896 because there was not sufficient demand for that type of product. Lotus Ware made during that short time period of five or six years is extremely prized by many collectors. Its acquisition is also not confined to American Belleek collectors. Because Lotus Ware was a bone china and technically not a Belleek-type porcelain, some American Belleek collectors do not include Lotus Ware as part of the American Belleek picture. The history of its development, however, is definitely linked to the Irish Belleek. Most references do refer to Lotus Ware as a type of Belleek because of its similarity in body and glaze to other American Belleek and because Lotus Ware was made during the American Belleek Era.

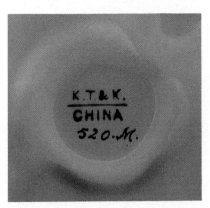

Knowles, Taylor & Knowles Mark 1. ''K.T. & K.'' initials over ''CHINA,'' ca. 1891 to 1896.

Knowles, Taylor & Knowles Mark 2. ''K.T.K. & Co'' printed with crescent and star inside circle with ''LOTUS WARE'' printed below, ca. 1891-1896.

PLATE 76. KTK Mark 2. Vase, 10″h, pedestal base, Art Nouveau shaped handles, applied jewelled medallions on each side under handles and at neck in front and back, beaded trim, dark green matte finish, gilded trim.

PLATE 77. Side view of vase in preceding photograph.

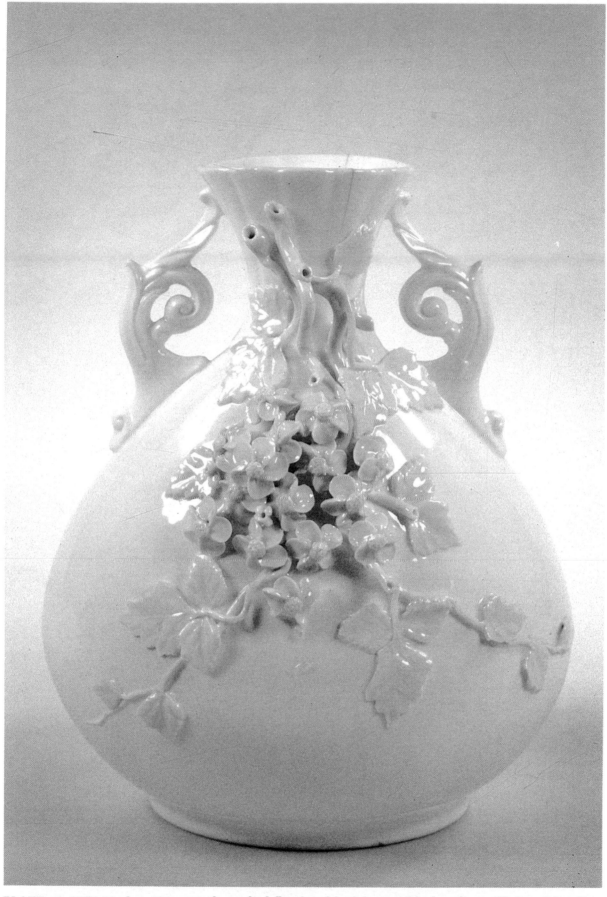

PLATE 78. KTK Mark 2. Vase, 8½″h, applied floral and leaf decor, ribbed neck, scroll-shaped handles.

PLATE 79. KTK Mark 2. Vase, 8½″h, handpainted violets with blue enamelling, gold paste work on neck, gilded handles and base.

PLATE 80. KTK Mark 2. Teapot, 5″h, applied "fishnet" work on body and lid, handpainted bows and gold paste designs, sponged gold on bamboo-shaped handle.

PLATE 81. KTK Mark 2. Pitcher, 5″h, same shape and "fishnet" work as teapot in Plate 80 with dainty floral designs.

PLATE 82. KTK Mark 2. Vase, 10″h, fancy applied handles, embossed designs on neck, scalloped base, artist signed "K.W.W., 1892."

PLATE 83. KTK Mark 2. Vase, 10″h, shape is similar to vase in Plate 76 (This particular shape was exhibited by Knowles, Taylor & Knowles at the Chicago Exposition in 1893), handpainted white and pink flowers on light green background, with bumblebee.

PLATE 84. KTK Mark 2. Small Jardiniere or Planter, 4¼″h, 4½″w, interior pink luster finish, embossed pink floral and gold leaf designs on body, scalloped border at top with beading.

PLATE 85. KTK Mark 2. Ewer, 10″h, same body shape as vase in Plate 83, pale yellow floral sprays, note that beaded work is not decorated.

PLATE 86. KTK Mark 2. Rose Jar, 7½″h, ornate open work on lid, pale blue floral sprays, gilded trim, artist signed on base "ASP '97."

PLATE 87. KTK Mark 1. Vase, 8½″h, 7″d, lily form with applied leaves and stems in an open-work design, deep pink and pale yellow matte finishes, gilded trim, artist signed on back with initial "M."

Lenox, Inc.

In 1906 the name of the Ceramic Art Company in Trenton, New Jersey, was changed to Lenox, Inc. to reflect Walter Lenox' sole ownership of the firm. Sometimes the Ceramic Art Company and the Lenox company are considered to be the same company because Walter Lenox was associated with both firms. Although the location and type of manufacture of the Ceramic Art Company did not change when the company name was changed to Lenox, the marks did change. Thus, for collectors, the Ceramic Art Company and Lenox, Inc., represent two different categories of American Belleek.

The new marks instituted in 1906 (see Lenox Marks 1 and 2) were similar to two of the CAC marks (compare CAC Marks 1 and 4). The letter "L" for "Lenox" was substituted for the "CAC" initials in both marks. The Lenox wreath mark was intended for factory decorated items, and the Lenox Belleek palette mark was designated for undecorated ware. Mark 1 was discontinued in 1924, and the wreath mark (Mark 2) was used for either factory decorated or undecorated porcelain. In 1930, "MADE IN U.S.A." was added to the Lenox wreath mark (Lenox, Inc., Information Sheet n.d.).

It is obvious that the wreath mark (Mark 2) did not include the word "Belleek," as the palette mark (Mark 1) did. Because the palette mark was discontinued in 1924, some collectors use that year as the cut-off date for classifying Lenox porcelain as American Belleek. The year 1930 is really a more accurate date. For reasons discussed in the first part of this book (see Historical Origins and Development of American Belleek), 1930 accurately marks the end of the American Belleek era. Although, the Lenox Belleek palette mark was not used after 1924, the Lenox wreath mark continued to be used until circa 1930 when the mark changed to include "Made in U.S.A." Therefore items with the Lenox wreath mark which do not have "Made in U.S.A." as part of the mark were, in all likelihood, made prior to 1930 (there could have been a short period of overlapping of marks after 1930), and should, of course, be classified as Lenox Belleek as well as pieces marked with the Lenox Belleek palette mark. If one confines collectible Lenox Belleek to only those items having the palette mark (and that is apparent in some cases), one is, in fact, limiting a collection to non-factory decorated items. On the other hand, if items having the wreath mark are included it is imposible to determine by the mark whether the pieces were made before or after 1924. Some information does show 1924 as the final year for the wreath mark, but that is incorrect because the wreath mark changed in 1930. That date is more accurate for separating Lenox Belleek from other Lenox porcelain made after that time. The date coincides nicely with the end of the American Belleek era.

Because of Lenox' continuous production over twenty-four years of factory decorated and white ware production, a large supply of both factory and non-factory decorated Lenox Belleek is available for collectors. The Lenox Company was in business much longer than all of the other American Belleek companies, except Willets. Thus, Lenox examples are not nearly so scarce as those of the other companies.

Lenox white ware decorated by professional artists is very desirable, and Lenox Belleek with sterling overlay work by American silver companies is increasingly in demand. Factory handpainted Lenox Belleek is more valuable than transfer decorated items. Pieces signed by Lenox factory artists are not readily available today, although the company employed quite a few artists. According to Robinson and Feeny (1980), Ceramic Art Company artists who continued working for Lenox, Inc., included Campana, DeLan, Marsh, George and William Morley, and Nosek. Two other Lenox decorators, Baker and Fenzel, are noted to have worked for the company after the name was changed to Lenox.

Before concluding this discussion of the Lenox company, a brief word should be included about its founder, Walter Scott Lenox, a native of Trenton, New Jersey. Lenox devoted his life to the potter's art. Although in 1895, he became blind and paralyzed in both legs, such severe handicaps did not keep him from his goal of showing that Americans could make quality porcelain and compete with foreign china companies. Walter Lenox died in 1920, but his company is still operating today which is obvious proof of his success. Walter Lenox did not invent American Belleek (as I discussed earlier in this book on the Origins of American Belleek), but his was the only company to not only survive but thrive with that type of porcelain production.

(For an interesting account of the life of Walter Lenox, see George Holmes, *Lenox China The Story of Walter Scott Lenox*, 1924. For an intensive study of the Ceramic Art Company and Lenox, Inc., see Robinson and Feeny, *The Official Price Guide to American Pottery & Porcelain, 1980.)*

Lenox Mark 1, initial "L" printed inside circle with artist's palette, "BELLEEK" printed below, usually in green, 1906 to 1924.

Lenox Mark 2, initial "L" printed inside Wreath, usually in green, 1906 to 1930.

PLATE 88. Lenox Mark 1. Bowl, 13″d, white ware, Dragon-shaped handles.

PLATE 90. Lenox Mark 1. Tea Set in "Hawthorn" body pattern: Teapot, 6½"h; Creamer, 3¾"h; Covered Sugar, 4¼"h.

PLATE 89. Lenox Mark 1. Candlesticks, white ware, raised scalloped designs on base.

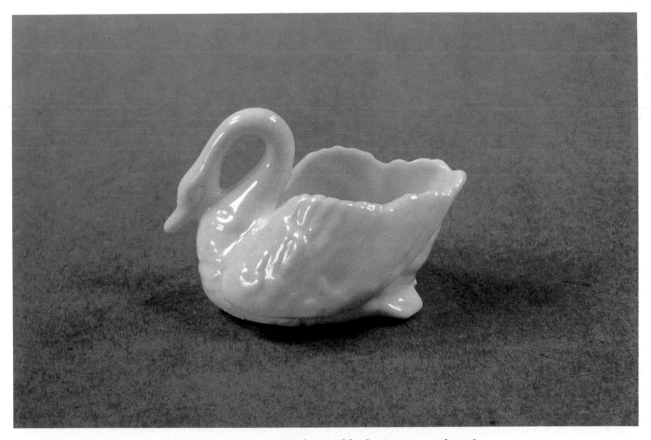

PLATE 91. Lenox Mark 2 in black. Swan, 1¾"h, 2"l.

PLATE 92. Lenox Mark 1. Vase, 13″h, handpainted Peacocks in Art Deco style, professional decoration.

PLATE 93. Lenox Mark 1 in black. Mug, 4½″h, hand-painted gooseberries in red, angular handle, artist sign-ed "Cline," non-professional decoration.

PLATE 94. Lenox Mark 1 in black. Mug, 4½″h, same shape as mug in preceding photograph, handpainted grapes, non-professional decoration.

PLATE 95. Lenox Mark 1. Vase, 6½″h, handpainted foliage in several shades of green, non-professional decoration.

PLATE 96. Lenox Mark 1. Talcum Shaker, 6″h, hand-painted rose garland with blue bow on pale blue background, gilded top, artist signed, non-professional decoration, scarce item.

PLATE 97. Lenox Mark 1. Commemorative Mug, 6½″h, parian body, handpainted blue and white scenic decor of girl canoeing. Inscription on back, "Salmagund Library Moving," professional decoration.

PLATE 98. Lenox Mark 1. Miniature vase, 3″h, handpainted flowers, non-professional decoration.

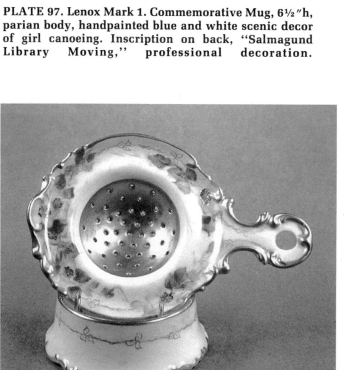

PLATE 99. Lenox Mark 1. Tea Strainer, 6″l, handpainted, artist signed on back, non-professional decoration, rare item.

PLATE 100. Lenox Mark 1. Jam Jar, 4″h, handpainted flowers with gold trim, non-professional decoration, scarce item.

PLATE 101. Lenox Mark 1. Vase, 8″h, note the shape rather than the decoration, elaborate figural handles, gilded trim, non-professionally hand-painted, unusual mold.

PLATE 102. Lenox Mark 1. Centerpiece Bowl on pedestal base, 4½″h, 9½″ from handle to handle, pink interior, handpainted roses, professional decoration.

PLATE 103. Lenox Mark 1. Centerpiece Bowl, 4½″h, 12″l, handpainted red tulips, gold trim with red accents, professional decoration.

PLATE 104. Lenox Mark 1. Square Dish, 5″sq., handpainted purple clematis blossoms with green leaves, gold trim, professional decoration.

PLATE 105. Lenox Mark 1. Vase, 16″h, handpainted red and white poppies, artist signed "E.S. Wilcox,"
professional decoration.

PLATE 106. Lenox Mark 1. Vase, 10″h, handpainted figural decor of two women, one in bridal dress, artist signed, professional decoration.

PLATE 107. Lenox Mark 2 in green, with "Marshall Fields" (Department Store). Set of six fish plates, handpainted and each signed by factory artist, W.H. Morley. The fish are identified on the back of each plate. "Brook Trout," and "Porgy," see following two photographs.

PLATE 108. Morley Fish Plates, "Weak Fish," and "Common Mackeral."

PLATE 109. Morley Fish Plates, "Pike," and "Sunfish."

PLATE 110. Lenox Mark 2 in green. Vase, 8¼″h, handpainted portrait of Springer Spaniel on front, artist signed "Baker," factory artist.

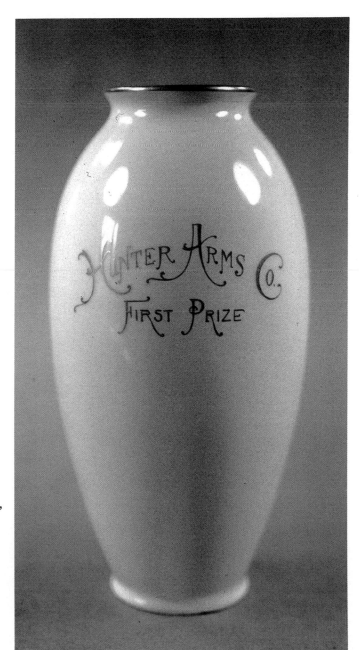

PLATE 111. Reverse side of Vase in preceding photograph, "Hunter Arms Co. First Prize," written in gold.

PLATE 112. Lenox Mark 1. Vase, 8¼h, handpainted figural scene of shepherdess and sheep, "Mt. St. Vincent" written on back, professional decoration.

PLATE 113. Lenox Mark 2 in green. Creamer, 6¼"h; Covered Sugar, 6"h, square pedestal base, angular handles, border design of single pink flowers and narrow gold lines, gold trim.

PLATE 114. Lenox Mark 1. Tea Set with sterling silver overlay in "Flying Geese" design with lake and trees including enamelled decoration of blue water and orange sunset. "Rockwell" mark on silver.

PLATE 115. Lenox Mark 2 in green. Individual Salts, 1½"h, gold band border in sterling silver holders.

PLATE 116. Lenox Mark 2 in green. Demi-tasse cup liner, gold band border, in Gorham sterling silver holder with saucer.

PLATE 117. Lenox Mark 1. Individual Chocolate Pot, 5¼"h, sterling silver overlay.

PLATE 118. Lenox Mark 1. Pitcher, 8"h, applied silver with floral cameo.

PLATE 119. Lenox Mark 1. Jam Jar, 5½"h, applied silver designs with handpainted floral cameo.

PLATE 120. Lenox Mark 1. Vase, 10″h, applied silver with handpainted floral cameo.

PLATE 121. Lenox Mark 1. Vase, 8½″h, 7½″w, applied silver with handpainted floral cameo.

PLATE 122. Lenox Mark 1. Coffee Pot, 11″h, applied silver with pink floral garlands and thin yellow enamell- ed horizontal lines.

Morgan Belleek China Company

A group of Canton, Ohio, investors founded a china company under the name of the Rea Company in 1923. The name of the firm was changed to the Morgan Belleek China Company in 1924. The renaming of the company reflected the name of the person in charge of production, William Morgan. Morgan had previously worked for the Lenox Company in Trenton, New Jersey (Heald, 1959). Morgan thus knew how to make Belleek porcelain, and this knowledge was put to use in making a very fine line of dinnerware which for a while competed successfully with the Lenox Belleek china.

Morgan Belleek dinnerware was beautifully decorated, and several different patterns were manufactured. Rich colors, especially deep maroon and cobalt blue, heavy gold trim, and hand enamelled designs were used. It is noted by Heald (1959) that complete sets ranged from $295.00 for the least expensive up to $1200.00 for cobalt and 24 karat gold decorated services. Morgan Belleek was definitely a luxury porcelain. When we see such prices from that time period, however, we must remember that the middle to late 1920s was a booming period in America's economy.

Although the Morgan Belleek China Company maintained a very good business, its operation ended in 1929 just after it had been taken over by the Ohio American China Corporation. During the same year, a suit which had been filed against the Morgan Belleek company by the Irish Belleek Pottery Limited, for using the name ''Belleek'' was decided in favor of the Irish company (Degenhardt, 1978). Thus after 1929, not only the Morgan company but other American china companies could not mark and market their porcelain legally as ''Belleek.'' That ruling plus competition with the Coxon Belleek Company (Wooster, Ohio) was instrumental in causing the Morgan Belleek Company to close.

The mark on Morgan Belleek china is a covered tureen with the words ''MORGAN'' printed above and ''BELLEEK'' printed below. Lehner (1983) shows two additional marks. One is similar to the mark I show, except that ''MORGAN'' and ''BELLEEK'' are written in script form. In another, the mark consists only of the words ''MORGAN'' over ''BELLEEK'' without the tureen, but with a pattern name, ''AZURE.'' Lehner notes that the second mark was granted a patent in 1929. Because that is the year the company closed, there may be few, if any, examples with that mark.

Morgan Belleek is quite rare, especially complete dinner services. Prices are similar for Morgan Belleek and for Coxon Belleek. They are more expensive than Lenox china made during the same time because those Ohio companies were in business for such a very short period.

Morgan Belleek China Mark in blue, ca. 1924 to 1929.

Morgan Belleek China Mark in green, ca. 1924 to 1929.

PLATE 123. Morgan Mark. Soup Plate for Dinner Service in photograph below.

PLATE 124. Morgan mark. Pieces to a Dinner Service decorated with a wide maroon border with blue and pink enamelled floral inserts. Dinner Plate, 11″d; Salad Plate (not shown), 8″d; Cup, 2½″h, Saucer, 6″d; Demi-tasse Cup, 2″h, Saucer, 4¾″d; Soup Plate, 8″d; Platter, 13″x8″.

Ott & Brewer

The Etruria Pottery was founded in 1863 by Bloor, Ott and Booth in Trenton, New Jersey. The name became Ott & Brewer after 1865, however, when John Hart Brewer joined the company (Barber, 1893). Ott & Brewer was the first America company to manufacture a Belleek porcelain. Their part in the development of this type of porcelain-making in America has been discussed in the first section of this book under "Historical Origins and Development of American Belleek."

Ott & Brewer manufactured American Belleek from circa 1883 to circa 1893 when the company closed. (The Cook Pottery Company took over the Ott & Brewer factory in 1894). During the ten-year period of Ott & Brewer's American Belleek production, a variety of fine quality art porcelain was produced. Many examples were similar to the Irish Belleek in type of object, form, and style of decoration. Other pieces were executed more in the style of the English Royal Worcester porcelains. The company also implemented original designs and decorations. Most of the pieces appear to be factory decorated, although occasionally, examples of non-factory decorated items are found. Information does not suggest that Ott & Brewer made a Belleek white ware line, and items which appear to be non-factory decorated may have escaped from the factory in various ways.

The primary marks associated with Ott & Brewer's "Belleek" porcelain are Marks 1 and 2. Mark 1 (a and b) is commonly known as the "Crown" mark, and Mark 2 as the "Crescent" mark. A variation of Mark 2 has "BELLEEK" rather than "TRENTON" writte inside the crescent shape (see Mark 3). The full name of the company (Marks 4 and 5) or just the initials "O." and "B." (see Mark 1b) may also be found on the firm's Belleek porcelain. The Crown and Crescent marks are usually found in red or brown, although one example had the Crescent mark in green. The colors of the marks do not appear to relate either to date or type of decoration.

Ott & Brewer American Belleek is especially important to collectors not only because the firm was the first to make "Belleek" porcelain in this country, but also because production lasted for only a short time. Examples are scarce, and many of the items are almost one hundred years old. Most importantly, the porcelain (in its body, design and decoration) illustrates the high artistic status the firm achieved during those ten years, thus making Ott & Brewer American Belleek especially coveted by collectors.

Ott & Brewer Mark 1a, Crown, initials, "BELLEEK," in brown, after 1883 to ca. 1893.

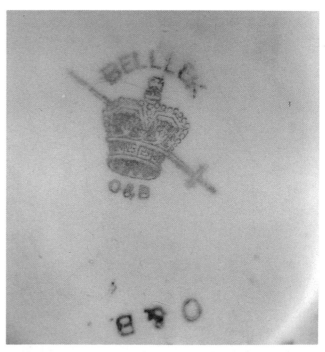

Ott & Brewer Mark 1b, Crown, initials, "BELLEEK," in red; note the "O" & "B" additional mark.

Ott & Brewer Mark 2, Crescent shape incorporating "O" and "B" initials with "TRENTON" printed inside Crescent, "BELLEEK" above, and "NJ" below, in red or green, after 1883 to ca. 1893.

Ott & Brewer Mark 3, Crescent shape incorporating "O" and "B" initials with "BELLEEK" printed inside Crescent, after 1883 and probably discontinued before or shortly after Mark 1.

Ott & Brewer Mark 4, full name of company printed in a circular shape, after 1883, to ca. 1893.

Ott & Brewer Mark 5, full name of company, after 1883 to ca. 1893.

PLATE 125. Ott & Brewer Marks 1 and 2. Small Bowl, 2"h, 4¾"d, scalloped border, gold paste floral and leaf designs on interior, embossed floral decoration on base. A transition piece showing both the Crown and Crescent marks.

PLATE 126. Base of Bowl in Plate 125 illustrating Crown and Crescent marks.

PLATE 127. Ott & Brewer Mark 1. Teapot, 8½″h, ornate tree-branch-style handle, handpainted red poppies with green leaves, gold outlining, bark finish at top and on spout, body mold has concave or "dented" design (lid is missing).

PLATE 128. Ott & Brewer Mark 2. Ewer, 8½″h, Cactus-shaped handle, gold paste stylized leaf decor on matte body finish.

PLATE 129. Ott & Brewer Mark 2. Ewer, 5¼"h, curved body design with top extending to form handle, gold paste floral and leaf decor on dimpled body.

PLATE 130. Ott & Brewer Mark 1. Watering pitcher, 8¾″h, gold paste floral and leaf decor, fancy applied ring-style handle, gilded trim.

PLATE 131. Ott & Brewer (unmarked). Teapot, 4½″h, Sugar, 4″h, Irish "Tridacna" body design, gold paste florals.

PLATE 132. Ott & Brewer Mark 2. Plate, 6¾″d, pink luster finish, gold trim.

PLATE 133. Ott & Brewer Mark 1. Pitcher, 8″h, gold paste thistle pattern on smooth body panel from spout to base, embossed and beaded designs on sides of pitcher, gilded trim.

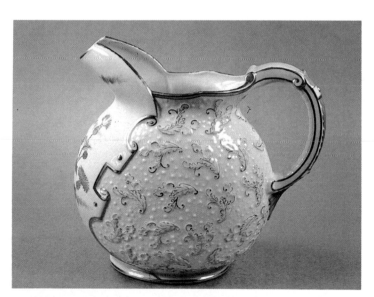

PLATE 134. Ott & Brewer Mark 1. Pitcher, 8″h, same shape as preceding pitcher, decoration extends to top of spout, and the embossed body designs are outlined in gold.

PLATE 135. Ott & Brewer Mark 1. Basket, 7½"h, 9"l, cactus-shaped handle with pink enamelled applied tulips, handpainted pink flowers and gold paste decor on body.

PLATE 136. Ott & Brewer Mark 1. Spherical-shaped vase, 7½"h, elaborate open work designs, applied tulips gilded with pink enamelled centers and long brown stems, applied gilded flowers and gold paste thistle pattern on body.

PLATE 137. Ott & Brewer Mark 2. Tray, 8″sq., handpainted scenic decor featuring a wild duck, deeply scalloped border, gilded knob feet on base.

PLATE 138. Ott & Brewer Mark 2. Vase, 4″h, 6″w, pinched at top to form three sections, deeply crimped border at top, gold paste floral decor on dark silvery background.

PLATE 139. Ott & Brewer Mark 1. Plate, 9″d, deeply scalloped border, gold paste stylized branch with leaves and berries.

PLATE 140. Ott & Brewer Mark 2. Cream Soup Cup, 2¾″h, 6″ handle to handle, Saucer, 7″d, gold paste work featuring a butterfly on each piece.

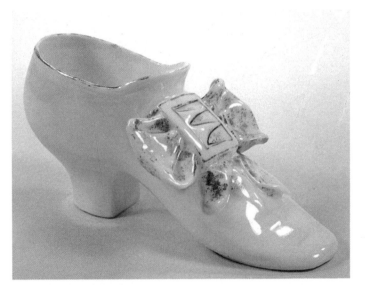

PLATE 141. Ott & Brewer Mark 2 in green and marked for the New Orleans Exhibition in 1885. Demi-tasse Cup, 2¾″h, pink luster finish interior of cup and center of saucer, enamelled pink floral sprays, gold trim.

PLATE 142. Ott & Brewer Mark 1. Shoe, 7½″l, sponged gold decor on applied bow on top of shoe.

PLATE 143. Ott & Brewer Mark 1. Bottle, 7½"h (lid missing), handpainted pink and gold flowers on one side, red flowers on the reverse (not shown), satin body finish.

PLATE 144. Ott & Brewer Mark 2. Vase, 10"h, handpainted pink flowers, gold paste leaves, matte body finish.

PLATE 145. Ott & Brewer Mark 1 in brown. Vase, 6½″h, double neck, applied twig handles, indented body, bark and matte finishes, gold paste floral and leaf designs.

PLATE 146. Ott & Brewer Mark 1. Vase, 6½″h, short pedestal base, gold paste floral and leaf designs, gold trim, matte body finish.

PLATE 147. Ott & Brewer Mark 1 on Individual Salt on right (see Cook Pottery for description of Salt on the left), 3 footed, multi-colored enamelled leaves and cattails.

PLATE 148. Ott & Brewer Marks 1 and 2. Sugar (Mark 2), 2″h, 3¼″d; Creamer (Mark 1), 3¼″h, deeply scalloped borders, pink and blue enamelled floral pattern.

PLATE 149. Ott & Brewer Mark 1. Ship's Vase, lily shape with wide rock-type base, applied leaf with silvery luster finish.

PLATE 150. Ott & Brewer Mark 2. Small Shell Compote, 3½″h, 5¾″d, supported on branch-formed pedestal base, pale blue luster finish.

PLATE 151. Ott & Brewer Mark 1. Tea Set, Irish "Tridacna" body design, handpainted pink flowers, bronze leaves, gold trim. Teapot, 5¾″h; Sugar, 4″h, Creamer, 3″h.

PLATE 152. Ott & Brewer Mark 2. Vase, 5½"h, gold paste leaf and butterfly pattern, matte body finish, beaded work around base of neck.

PLATE 153. Ott & Brewer Mark 1. Rose Jar, 5½"h, embossed floral designs on body, gold paste floral and leaf decor, satin body finish, intricately pierced top.

PLATE 154. Ott & Brewer Mark 1. Small Jardiniere, 4½"h, gold paste leaves, sponged gold on handles, matte body finish.

PLATE 155. Ott & Brewer Mark 1. Vase, 10¼"h, short neck, gold paste flowers and leaves, matte body finish.

PLATE 156. Ott & Brewer Mark 1. Pitcher, 6½″h, Horn-shaped, tree-branch style handle, bark finish on base in brown and gold, floral designs in gold paste on upper body, matte finish.

PLATE 157. Ott & Brewer (unmarked). Cup, 1¾″h; Saucer, 5½″d, handpainted red flowers with gold paste leaves and pale lavender sprigs.

PLATE 158 . Ott & Brewer Mark 1. Pedestal Tray with six circular openings, probably to hold eggs. Ornate handle patterned after the Irish "Dolphin" style.

PLATE 159. Ott & Brewer Mark 1. Cup, 2½″h, Saucer, 5½″d, gold paste floral, leaf and butterfly decor.

PLATE 160. Ott & Brewer Mark 2. Footed Shell Dish, 2½″h, 5¼″d, purple luster interior, the shell-shaped feet resemble the Irish "Neptune" design.

PLATE 161. Ott & Brewer Mark 1. Ram's Horn, 5½"w, pink luster finish, gold trim at top, a particularly rare item.

PLATE 162. Ott & Brewer Mark 1. Chocolate Pot, 13"h, designed with Dragon-shaped spout and handle, handpainted yellow flower with green leaves on white satin body finish, body design on lower third of pot has handpainted yellow decor, gilded trim with some wear on spout, artist signed on back "Kate, 1890," professional but not factory decoration.

PLATE 163. Ott & Brewer Mark 1. Cup, 2½"h, Saucer, 5½"d, gold paste floral and leaf decor.

PLATE 164. Ott & Brewer Mark 1. Bowl, 3½"h, 9¾"d, deeply scalloped border with sponged gold work, overlapping circular pattern on body, gold paste leaf designs on interior and exterior.

Perlee, Inc.

The Trenton, New Jersey, firm of Perlee, Inc., made a Belleek-type porcelain beginning in the 1920s until about 1930. Lehner (1980) says the company was listed in the Trenton City Directories from 1926 to 1930. Other information suggests a somewhat longer period of eight to ten years during the same approximate time of the early 1920s. (See "Collecting American Belleek" in the first part of this book for more discussion about the Perlee Company.)

The mark of the firm includes the letter "P" in a wreath with "PERLEE INC." and "TRENTON BELEEK" written underneath. Note that "Beleek" was spelled with only one "L."

Decorated dinnerware and decorative items are found with Perlee marks. Undecorated porcelain or white ware probably was not sold because the china painting hobby was just about out of fashion by the time Perlee would have started production. The design of Perlee Beleek is similar to that made by the Ohio companies of Morgan Belleek and Coxon Belleek, having smooth or plain shapes. The quality of the porcelain and the decoration are not as fine however. Few Perlee examples are available, but the prices are considerably lower than prices for either Coxon or Morgan products.

Perlee Mark, "P" in a wreath, "PERLEE TRENTON BELEEK" printed below, ca. mid 1920s to ca. 1930.

PLATE 165. Perlee Mark, Vase, 5″h, Black border at top with multi-colored florals, gold trim.

PLATE 166. Perlee Mark, Tea Set, peacock decor: Teapot, 5½″h, 10″ from spout to handle; Covered Sugar, 4″h; Creamer, 3¾″h.

Willets Manufacturing Company

Three brothers, Joseph, Daniel, and Edmund Willets founded Willets Manufacturing Company in Trenton, New Jersey, in 1879. The company remained in business for over thirty years. During that time many different types of pottery were made, but Willets is best known for its Belleek porcelain. The exact date when the company started making Belleek is not clear, but it had to be after 1883, and probably was sometime in 1884 or 1885. Barber (1893) states that William Bromley, Sr., who had come to Trenton from the Irish Belleek factory in 1883 to help Ott & Brewer in perfecting the Belleek process, left that company after he ". . . got it well under way," and started to work for Willets to teach them the technique. Most sources agree that Willets manufactured Belleek until about 1909, a period of twenty-four or twenty-five years.

Willets used several different marks on its various types of ware. Their mark on Belleek porcelain was printed in the form of a twisted Serpent with "WILLETS" printed below (see Mark 1). Another version of that mark has "BELLEEK" printed above the Serpent (see Mark 2). Presumably Mark 1 (without "BELLEEK") is the earlier of the two marks, but Mark 2 is the one seen more frequently.

The Willets mark may be in red, brown, black, blue, or green. Barber (1893) indicated that the mark in red was for factory decorated Belleek items. In another of his books, (Barber, 1904), he says only that the Willets Serpent mark was overglaze in red, brown, and black. He does not say whether the mark was on factory or non-factory decorated ware, and he did not mention a green or blue color for the mark.

The blue mark does not present much of a problem because it is found only on the company's factory decorated "Delft-style" items. The red, brown, or black marks may be found on factory decorated pieces, but the brown and black marks also appear on non-factory decorated objects. My theory is that the company probably did not sell undecorated porcelain at first. When it began to do so, the red mark was reserved for factory decorated articles, and the brown or black marks were still used on either white ware or decorated ware. At some point, however, the company decided to mark all white ware in green. It was the custom for European white ware, which was being imported during that time, to be factory marked in green. It would thus seem reasonable for American companies to adopt that practice. This, logically, would make the green mark later than the other colors. It is clear that the practice of marking white ware in green was adopted by some companies. For example, the Ceramic Art Company palette mark was used in several colors on both factory and non-factory decorated pieces, but the white ware of Lenox, which succeeded CAC, is primarily marked in green. Willets examples with the green mark shown here all appear to have non-factory decoration by either amateur artists, professional artists, or silver companies, or no decoration at all (white ware).

The Willets Manufacturing Company was quite successful for a long time in making American Belleek. Its twenty-four or twenty-five year period compares in length to that of the Lenox porcelain made during the American Belleek era. For its age, Willets rates higher than Lenox in the collectible hierarchy. Willets Belleek is not so rare as Ott & Brewer Belleek, although Willets began making Belleek shortly after Ott & Brewer. Willets was in business over twice as long as Ott & Brewer, and thus more Willets Belleek was made and is available.

In contrast to Ott & Brewer, whose available Belleek is primarily factory decorated, a very large amount of Willets Belleek consists of non-factory decorated objects. Prices for Willets factory decorated Belleek, especially those similar to Ott & Brewer items and the Irish Belleek, command the highest prices. Non-factory decorated articles show a wide price differential depending on the quality of the art work, and usually are comparable in price to European white ware decorated in this country during the same time period. The better the quality of decoration, the higher the price. Few factory decorated artist-signed examples are found. George and Oliver Houghton, Nosek, Renelt, and With are listed by Robinson and Feeny (1980) as artists who worked for Willets. Walter Lenox was also associated with Willets before he and Jonathan Coxon became partners in the Ceramic Art Company.

Willets Mark 1. Serpent without "BELLEEK," exact date unknown, but probably toward middle 1880s and prior to Mark 2.

Willets Mark 2. Serpent with "BELLEEK," ca. middle 1880s to ca. 1909.

PLATE 167. Willets Mark 2 in brown. Vase, 12″h, elaborate open work with floral designs, scalloped footed base, handpainted red and gold flowers, matte finish, gilded trim.

PLATE 168. Willets Mark 2 in brown. Muffineer, 4½"h, undecorated.

PLATE 169. Unmarked. but attributed to Willets. Bowl, 2¾"h, 9"d, ornately scalloped border, undecorated.

PLATE 170. Willets Mark 2 in brown. Individual Salt, 1¾"h, heart shaped, scalloped border, undecorated.

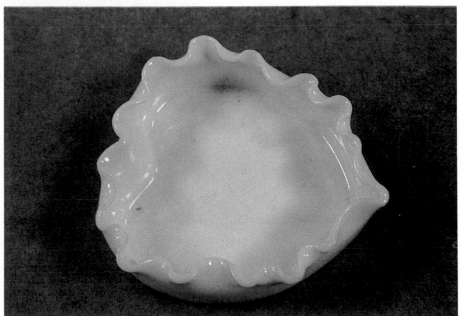

PLATE 171. Willets Mark 2 in green. Centerpiece, 12½″l, each section connected with shell-shaped foot, gold trim, professional decoration.

PLATE 172. Willets Mark 2 in brown. Individual Salts, 1½″h, crimped border, enamelled flowers.

PLATE 173. Willets Mark 2 in brown. Portrait Mug, 5¾"h, handpainted cherub on one side and young woman on the other (see Plate 174), factory artist signed ''H. Nosek.''

PLATE 174. Reverse view of Mug in Plate 173.

PLATE 175. Unmarked, but attributed to Willets. Chamberstick, 5″h, an extremely ornate design combining applied flowers and spaghetti-type work in the Irish Belleek style.

PLATE 176. Willets Mark 1 in red. Pitchers, "Cane" body design, lavender tint with gold sponged work, handles designed in overlapping fashion, gilded. Left, 7″h; Right, 3¼″h.

PLATE 177. Willets Mark 2 in black. Vase, 14″h, handpainted large pink and red roses, handles, border of neck and base decorated with gold, professional decoration.

PLATE 178. Willets Mark 2 in green. Vase, 13″h, handpainted roses, artist signed "Marsh," professional decoration. (Marsh worked as an artist for Lenox, but this example with a green Willets mark indicates that the artist also painted other firms' white ware.)

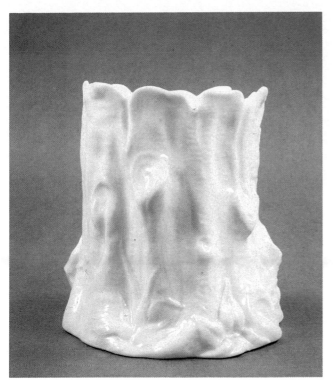

PLATE 179. Unmarked, but attributed to Willets. Tree Trunk Vase, 5″h.

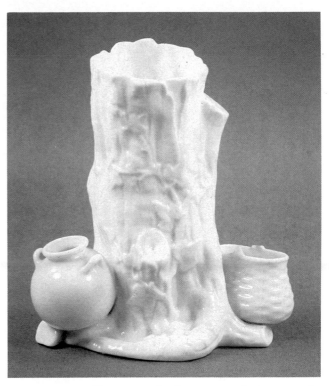

PLATE 180. Willets (unmarked). Tree Trunk Vase, 6½″h, applied pot and basket (handle missing on basket).

PLATE 181. Miniatures by Willets, Clockwise, left to right: Loving Cup, Mark 2 in green, handpainted blue floral decor, 1¾″h; Vase, Mark 2 in green, undecorated, 1¾″h; Chalice, Mark 2 in brown, Indian Portrait "Oguntz," 2½″h; Pair of Vases, Mark 2 in brown, undecorated, 2¾″h; Vase, Mark 2 in green, handpainted blue flowers, 2¾″h; Mug, Mark 2 in brown, undecorated, 1¾″h; Jardiniere, Mark 2 in brown, handpainted roses and beaded work, 2¼″h; Basket, unmarked, lotus blossom shape (center), undecorated, 2½″l. Only the jardiniere and chalice are factory decorated.

**PLATE 182. Willets Mark 2 in brown. Vase, 18½″h, handpainted portrait of a child, signed "J. Nosek,"
factory artist.**

PLATE 183. Willets Mark 2 in red. Footed Bowl, 2″h, 6″l, small reserve of handpainted roses, outlined with beaded border and small floral designs in gold.

PLATE 184. Unmarked, but attributed to Willets. Plates, 8¾″d, transfer cupid and cherub decor, deeply scalloped borders brushed with gold, tinted blue-grey background.

PLATE 185. Willets Mark 2 in brown. Loving Cup, 8″h, pedestal base, handpainted angels, gilded designs and monogram on base, professional decoration.

PLATE 186. Willets Mark 2 in brown. Cup, 3¾″h, 4½″d, pedestal base; Saucer, 6″d, handpainted portrait medallions, gold enamelled line and scroll designs, professional decoration.

PLATE 187. Willets Mark 2 in brown. Vase, 20½″h, hand-painted chrysanthemums, Art Deco style angular handles and neck, professional decoration.

PLATE 188. Willets Mark 2 in green. Vase, 12¾″h, smaller version of vase in Plate 187, sterling silver decor.

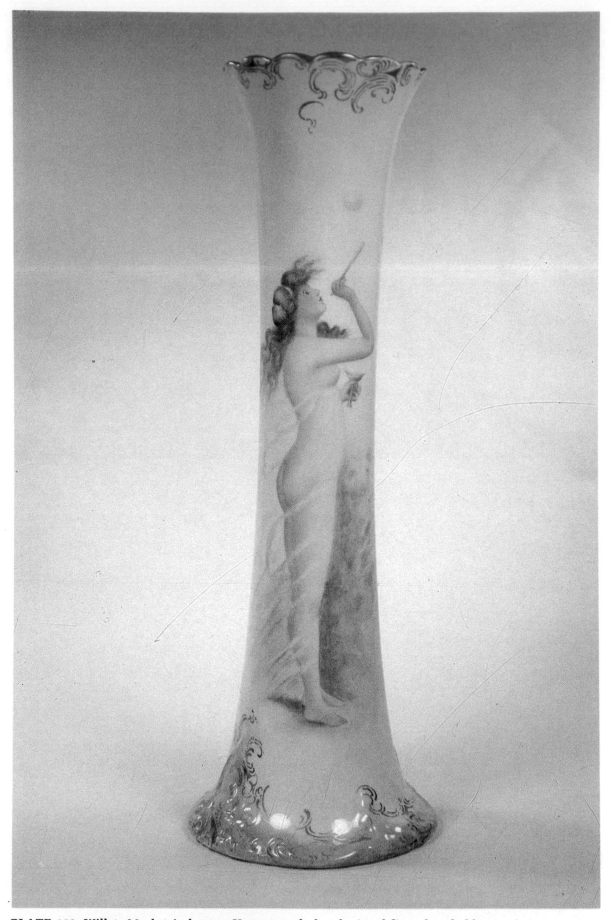

PLATE 189. Willets Mark 2 in brown. Vase, 15½″h, handpainted figural nude blowing bubbles, tinted lavender background, professional decoration.

PLATE 190. Willets Mark 2 in brown. Open Sugar, fancy crimped border, gold paste scroll and leaf designs, tiny pink enamelled flowers on interior and exterior, artist signed "RE."

PLATE 191. Unmarked, but attributed to Willets. Tea Set: Teapot, 6″h; Sugar, 4¼″h; Creamer, 3¼″h, "Coral" shaped handles, shell finials, pink tinted finish.

PLATE 192. Willets Mark 2 in brown. Clock, 13½″h, scroll and leaf designs in gold with tiny pink enamell-ed flowers.

PLATE 193. Willets Mark 2 in brown. Coffee Pot, 8″h, square pedestal base, silver decor, professional decoration.

PLATE 194. Willets Mark 2 in green. Bowl, 3″h, 7½″d, turned down rim, platinum resist work on border, professional decoration.

PLATE 195. Willets Mark 2 in red. Creamer, 3¾″h, top fashioned in 4 sections by large scallops, one forming spout, twisted rope style handle, gold paste floral and leaf decoration, matte body finish.

PLATE 196. Willets Mark 2 in red. Pitcher, 5¼″h, crimped border, body indentation, tree-branch shaped handle, pink and gold paste floral decor.

PLATE 197. Willets Mark 2 in brown. Covered Sugar, 7″h, square pedestal base, undecorated.

PLATE 198. Willets Mark 2 in brown. Creamer, 7″h, square pedestal base, undecorated.

PLATE 199. Willets Mark 2 in green. Creamer 3¾″h, same shape as creamer in Plate 195 but undecorated.

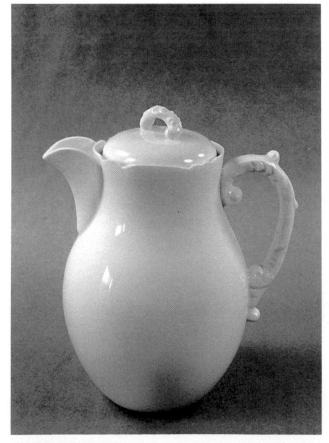

PLATE 200. Willets Mark 2 in brown. Chocolate Pot, 9″h, undecorated.

PLATE 201. Willets Mark 2 in brown. Ring Tree, 4½″h, tiny flowers, brushed gold trim, rare item.

PLATE 202. Willets Mark 1 in red. Egg Cup, 2¾″h, petal design.

PLATE 203. Willets Mark 2 in black. Vase, 15″h, 10″w, handpainted birds, high glaze finish, professional decoration.

PLATE 204. Willets Mark 2 in brown. Vase, 17″h, handpainted bird decor on front, tree limbs and leaves on back, high glaze finish, professional decoration.

PLATE 205. Willets Mark 2 in brown. Teapot, 4½"h, handpainted blue flowers on body, gold trim, lid undecorated, non-professional decoration.

PLATE 206. Willets Mark 2 in brown. Pitcher, 5"h, crimped border, fancy handle, violets, gold trim.

PLATE 207. Willets Mark 2 in brown. Vase, 10½"h, handpainted flowers with purple berries, artist signed on base with the year "'08," non-professional decoration.

PLATE 208. Willets Mark 2 in brown. Vase, 15"h, 8"d at top, handpainted purple and green grapes, artist signed "ERS Williams," non-professional decoration.

PLATE 209. Willets Mark 2 in brown. Pitcher, 6½″h, handpainted blackberries, embossed work on handle and base, non-professional decoration.

PLATE 210. Willets Mark 2 in brown. Mug, 6″h, dragon-shaped handle, handpainted, non-professional decoration (dragon shaped handles are popular).

PLATE 211. Willets Mark 2 in black. Tankard, 13″h, dragon-shaped handle, handpainted flowers with grey foliage on tinted brown background, professional decoration.

PLATE 212. Willets Mark 2 in brown.Pitcher, 9½″h, small pink and blue enamelled floral garlands with gold leaves, pale green and pink tinted body, gilded trim.

PLATE 213. Willets Mark 2 in brown. Chalice, 11½"h, Art Nouveau style decoration with handpainted gold grapes on black background, artist signed "Hessler," Pickard artist (Pickard Decorating Mark on base in addition to Willets Mark).

PLATE 214. Willets Mark 2 in brown. Chalice, 11½"h, handpainted red berries, green leaves, gold trim, artist signed, professional decoration.

PLATE 215. Willets Mark 2 in brown. Chalice, 11½″h, handpainted, Monk smoking cigar, brown tones, artist signed "AHP," professional decoration.

Bibliography

Barber, Edwin Atlee. *The Pottery and Porcelain of the United States*, with supplements, (1893 and 1901) and *Marks of American Potters* (1904). Combined edition published by Feingold & Lewis, distributed by J & J Publishing, New York, Bicentennial Limited edition.

"Belleek Porcelain," *The Encyclopedia of Collectibles*. Alexandria, Virginia: Time-Life Books, 1978.

Boger, Louis Ade. *The Dictionary of World Pottery and Porcelain*. New York: Charles Scribner's Sons, 1971.

Cole, Ann Kilborn. *How to Collect the "New" Antiques*. New York: David McKay Company, Inc., 1966.

Degenhardt, Richard K. *Belleek: The Complete Collector's Guide and Illustrated Reference*. Huntington, New York: Portfolio Press, 1978.

Evans, Paul. *Art Pottery of the United States*. Hanover, Pennsylvania: Everybodys Press, Inc., 1974.

Gatchell, Dana King. *Know Your Tablewares*. Ann Arbor, Michigan: Edwards Brothers, Inc., 1944.

Heald, Edward Thorton. *The Stark County Story*. Columbus, Ohio: Stark County Historical Society, 1959.

Holmes, George Sanford. *Lenox China: The Story of Walter Scott Lenox*, Trenton, New Jersey: Lenox, Inc., 1924.

Hudgeons, Thomas E., III (ed.), *The Official 1983 Price Guide to Pottery & Porcelain*. Orlando, Florida: House of Collectibles, 1983.

Ketchum, William C., Jr. *The Pottery and Porcelain Collector's Handbook*. New York: Funk & Wagnalls, 1971.

Lenox-China. White Ware Catalog, 1922.

Lenox Marks Information Sheet. Lenox Incorporated, Trenton, New Jersey, n.d.

Lehner, Lois. *Ohio Pottery and Glass Marks and Manufacturers.* Des Moines, Iowa: Wallace-Homestead Book Co., 1978.

————. *Complete Book of American Kitchen and Dinner Wares*. Des Moines, Iowa: Wallace-Homestead Book Co., 1980.

————. "Research on American Belleek: Coxon and Morgan," *The Antique Trader,* June 29, 1983.

Markham, Kenneth H. "Coxon and Morgan Belleek China," *The Antiques Journal,* September, 1962.

Reilly, Anna D. "American Belleek," *Spinning Wheel*, June, 1952.

Robinson, Dorothy and Bill Feeny. *The Official Price Guide to American Pottery & Porcelain.* Orlando, Florida: House of Collectibles, 1980.

Schroeder's Antiques Price Guide. Paducah, Kentucky: Collector Books, 1983.

Schwartz, Marvin D. *Collectors' Guide to Antique American Ceramics*. Garden City, New York: Doubleday & Company, Inc., 1969.

Schwartz, Marvin D. and Suzanne Boorsch. *19th-Century America Furniture and other Decorative Arts.* New York: The Metropolitan Museum of Art, 1970.

Schwartz, Marvin D. and Betsy Wade. *The New York Times Book of Antiques*. New York: Quadrangle Books, 1972.

Schwartz, Marvin D. and Richard Wolfe. *A History of American Art Porcelain.* New York: Renaissance Editions, 1967.

Webster's New World Dictionary. New York: Simon and Schuster, 1982.

Object Index

American Belleek Value Guide

American Art China Works
Plate 1. $1200.00-1400.00 pair
Plate 2. $100.00-125.00
Plate 3. $200.00-250.00
Plate 4. Open Sugar, $150.00-200.00; Creamer, $175.00-225.00
Plate 5. $175.00-225.00
Plate 6. $300.00-350.00

American Beleek Company, Inc.
Plate 7. $100.00-150.00
Plate 8. $75.00-100.00

Beleek
Plate 9. $400.00-500.00
Plate 10. $50.00-75.00

Ceramic Art Company
Plate 11. $1000.00-1200.00
Plate 12. $250.00-300.00
Plate 13. $100.00-125.00
Plate 14. Inkwell, $60.00-80.00; Blotter Corners, $100.00-125.00 pair; Blotter, $125.00-150.00
Plate 15. $175.00-200.00
Plate 16. $45.00-55.00
Plate 17. $50.00-60.00 set
Plate 18. $150.00-200.00 each
Plate 19. $75.00-100.00
Plate 20. $700.00-800.00
Plate 21. $400.00-500.00
Plate 22. $600.00-700.00
Plate 23. $900.00-1000.00
Plate 24. $450.00-550.00
Plate 25. $450.00-500.00
Plate 26. $350.00-450.00
Plate 27. (see Plate 26)
Plate 28. (see Plate 26)
Plate 29. Left, $300.00-350.00; Right, $225.00-275.00
Plate 30. $75.00-125.00
Plate 31. $125.00-175.00
Plate 32. $175.00-225.00 each
Plate 33. Hairbrush, $175.00-200.00; Hand Mirror, $225.00-250.00; Nail Buffer Base, $100.00-125.00
Plate 34. $500.00-600.00
Plate 35. $400.00-500.00
Plate 36. $300.00-350.00

Plate 37. $75.00-100.00 set
Plate 38. $35.00-45.00
Plate 39. $125.00-150.00
Plate 40. $150.00-200.00
Plate 41. $300.00-350.00
Plate 42. $1000.00-1200.00
Plate 43. $425.00-475.00
Plate 44. $600.00-700.00
Plate 45. $125.00-150.00
Plate 46. (see Plate 45)
Plate 47. $300.00-350.00
Plate 48. $200.00-250.00
Plate 49. $125.00-150.00
Plate 50. $75.00-100.00
Plate 51. $75.00-100.00
Plate 52. Swan Salt $40.00-50.00; Spoon $150.00-175.00
Plate 53. $600.00-700.00
Plate 54. $100.00-125.00
Plate 55. $150.00-175.00
Plate 56. $100.00-125.00
Plate 57. $150.00-200.00
Plate 58. $400.00-450.00
Plate 59. $100.00-125.00
Plate 60. $125.00-150.00
Plate 61. $200.00-250.00
Plate 62. $125.00-150.00
Plate 63. $300.00-350.00
Plate 64. $550.00-650.00

Columbian Art Pottery
Plate 65. $200.00-250.00
Plate 66. $250.00-300.00
Plate 67. $400.00-500.00
Plate 68. $80.00-100.00
Plate 69. $800.00-1000.00

Cook Pottery Company
Plate 70. $125.00-150.00

Coxon Belleek Pottery
Plate 71. $150.00-200.00 each
Plate 72. $100.00-150.00 each
Plate 73. Creamer, $250.00-300.00; Covered Sugar, $250.00-300.00; Teapot, $400.00-500.00; Bread & Butter Plate, $50.00-75.00; Cup and Saucer, $150.00-200.00

Gordon Belleek
Plate 74. $40.00-50.00
Plate 75. $75.00-100.00 each

Knowles, Taylor & Knowles
Plate 76. $900.00-1000.00
Plate 77. (see Plate 76)
Plate 78. $800.00-900.00
Plate 79. $700.00-800.00
Plate 80. $600.00-700.00
Plate 81. $550.00-650.00
Plate 82. $500.00-600.00
Plate 83. $500.00-600.00
Plate 84. $400.00-500.00
Plate 85. $550.00-650.00
Plate 86. $650.00-750.00
Plate 87. $800.00-900.00

Lenox, Inc.
Plate 88. $100.00-125.00
Plate 89. $125.00-150.00 pair
Plate 90. $150.00-200.00 set
Plate 91. $25.00-30.00
Plate 92. $300.00-350.00
Plate 93. $75.00-100.00
Plate 94. $75.00-100.00
Plate 95. $50.00-60.00
Plate 96. $100.00-125.00
Plate 97. $175.00-200.00
Plate 98. $75.00-100.00
Plate 99. $225.00-275.00
Plate 100. $75.00-100.00
Plate 101. $150.00-200.00
Plate 102. $150.00-175.00
Plate 103. $100.00-125.00
Plate 104. $50.00-60.00
Plate 105. $300.00-400.00
Plate 106. $500.00-600.00
Plate 107. $700.00-800.00 set of 6
Plate 108. (see Plate 107)
Plate 109. (see Plate 107)
Plate 110. $450.00-550.00
Plate 111. (see Plate 110)
Plate 112. $400.00-500.00
Plate 113. $125.00-150.00 set
Plate 114. $500.00-600.00 set
Plate 115. $40.00-50.00 each
Plate 116. $65.00-75.00 each
Plate 117. $150.00-175.00

Plate 118. $425.00-525.00
Plate 119. $200.00-250.00
Plate 120. $400.00-500.00
Plate 121. $450.00-550.00
Plate 122. $500.00-600.00

Morgan Belleek China Company
Plate 123. $150.00-200.00
Plate 124. Plate, $175.00-225.00; Salad Plate, $80.00-100.00; Cup and Saucer, $150.00-200.00; Demi-tasse Cup and Saucer, $175.00-200.00; Platter, $250.00-300.00

Ott & Brewer
Plate 125. $350.00-400.00
Plate 126. (see Plate 125)
Plate 127. $550.00-650.00
Plate 128. $800.00-900.00
Plate 129. $400.00-500.00
Plate 130. $600.00-700.00
Plate 131. Sugar, $200.00-250.00; Teapot, $350.00-450.00
Plate 132. $75.00-100.00
Plate 133. $500.00-600.00
Plate 134. $550.00-650.00
Plate 135. $800.00-900.00
Plate 136. $900.00-1000.00
Plate 137. $600.00-700.00
Plate 138. $650.00-750.00
Plate 139. $250.00-300.00
Plate 140. $250.00-300.00
Plate 141. $250.00-300.00
Plate 142. $500.00-600.00
Plate 143. $500.00-600.00
Plate 144. $600.00-700.00
Plate 145. $500.00-600.00
Plate 146. $400.00-500.00
Plate 147. $100.00-125.00
Plate 148. $350.00-400.00 set

Plate 149. $900.00-1000.00
Plate 150. $300.00-350.00
Plate 151. $800.00-900.00 set
Plate 152. $400.00-500.00
Plate 153. $600.00-700.00
Plate 154. $350.00-400.00
Plate 155. $600.00-700.00
Plate 156. $650.00-750.00
Plate 157. $75.00-100.00
Plate 158. $550.00-650.00
Plate 159. $225.00-275.00
Plate 160. $150.00-200.00
Plate 161. $1500.00-2000.00
Plate 162. $600.00-700.00
Plate 163. $150.00-175.00
Plate 164. $700.00-800.00

Perlee, Inc.
Plate 165. $75.00-100.00
Plate 166. $300.00-400.00 set

Willets Manufacturing Company
Plate 167. $800.00-1000.00
Plate 168. $70.00-80.00
Plate 169. $45.00-55.00
Plate 170. $12.00-15.00
Plate 171. $75.00-100.00
Plate 172. $30.00-40.00 each
Plate 173. $800.00-1000.00
Plate 174. (see Plate 173)
Plate 175. $300.00-350.00
Plate 176. Pitchers, 7″, $150.00-200.00; 3¼″, $75.00-100.00
Plate 177. $600.00-700.00
Plate 178. $600.00-700.00
Plate 179. $150.00-175.00
Plate 180. $200.00-250.00
Plate 181. Loving Cup, $125.00-150.00; Vase, $125.00-150.00;

Chalice, $150.00-175.00; Pair of Vases, $125.00-150.00 each; Vase, $125.00-150.00; Mug, $125.00-150.00; Jardiniere, $150.00-175.00; Basket, $100.00-125.00
Plate 182. $1200.00-1500.00
Plate 183. $80.00-100.00
Plate 184. $350.00-400.00 pair
Plate 185. $400.00-450.00
Plate 186. $350.00-450.00
Plate 187. $350.00-400.00
Plate 188. $300.00-350.00
Plate 189. $800.00-1000.00
Plate 190. $150.00-175.00
Plate 191. $300.00-350.00 set
Plate 192. $650.00-750.00
Plate 193. $150.00-200.00
Plate 194. $100.00-125.00
Plate 195. $150.00-175.00
Plate 196. $150.00-175.00
Plate 197. $40.00-50.00
Plate 198. $40.00-50.00
Plate 199. $30.00-40.00
Plate 200. $50.00-75.00
Plate 201. $200.00-250.00
Plate 202. $150.00-200.00
Plate 203. $600.00-700.00
Plate 204. $400.00-500.00
Plate 205. $40.00-50.00
Plate 206. $50.00-75.00
Plate 207. $125.00-175.00
Plate 208. $150.00-200.00
Plate 209. $75.00-100.00
Plate 210. $100.00-125.00
Plate 211. $300.00-400.00
Plate 212. $300.00-350.00
Plate 213. $400.00-500.00
Plate 214. $400.00-500.00
Plate 215. $500.00-600.00

Two Important Tools For The
Astute Antique Dealer, Collector and Investor

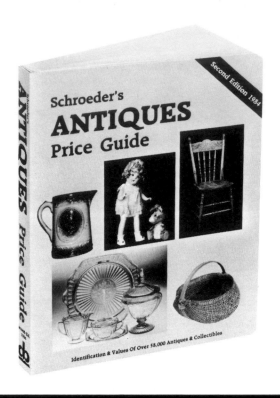

Schroeder's Antiques Price Guide

The very best low cost investment that you can make if you are really serious about antiques and collectibles is a good identification and price guide. We publish and highly recommend **Schroeder's Antiques Price Guide.** Our editors and writers are very careful to seek out and report accurate values each year. We do not simply change the values of the items each year but start anew to bring you an entirely new edition. If there are repeats, they are by chance and not by choice. Each huge edition (it weighs 3 pounds!) has over 56,000 descriptions and current values on 608 - 8½x11 pages. There are hundreds and hundreds of categories and even more illustrations. Each topic is introduced by an interesting discussion that is an education in itself. Again, no dealer, collector or investor can afford not to own this book. It is available from your favorite bookseller or antiques dealer at the low price of $9.95. If you are unable to find this price guide in your area, it's available from Collector Books, P. O. Box 3009, Paducah, KY 42001 at $9.95 plus $1.00 for postage and handling.

Schroeder's INSIDER and Price Update

A monthly newsletter published for the antiques and collectibles marketplace.

The **"INSIDER"**, as our subscribers have fondly dubbed it, is a monthly newsletter published for the antiques and collectibles marketplace. It gives the readers timely information as to trends, price changes, new finds, and market moves both upward and downward. Our writers are made up of a panel of well-known experts in the fields of Glass, Pottery, Dolls, Furniture, Jewelry, Country, Primitives, Oriental and a host of other fields in our huge industry. Our subscribers have that "inside edge" that makes them more profitable. Each month we explore 8-10 subjects that are "in", and close each discussion with a random sampling of current values that are recorded at press time. Thousands of subscribers eagerly await each monthly issue of this timely 16-page newsletter. A sample copy is available for $3.00 postpaid. Subscriptions are $24.00 for 12 months; 24 months for $45.00; 36 months for $65.00, all postpaid. A sturdy 3-ring binder to store your **Insider** is available for $5.00 postpaid. This newsletter contains NO paid advertising and is not available on your newsstand. It may be ordered by sending your check or money order to Collector Books, P. O. Box 3009, Paducah, KY 42001.

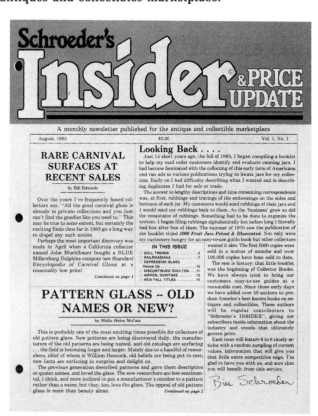